Hiking Trails of the

BOULDER

MOUNTAIN AREA

NEW EDITION

Hiking Trails of the

BOULDER

MOUNTAIN AREA

Vici De Haan

ISBN: 0-87108-531-3

Library of Congress Catalog Card No. 79-87492

Second Edition
1 2 3 4 5 6 7 8 9
Printed in the United States of America

Contents

Preface

How many people realize the wealth of hiking trails that are available to them right here in our own back yard? As a native of Boulder, I have spent many glorious hours tromping through these foothills and would like to share my enjoyment of the out-of-doors with any others who also enjoy hiking.

All trails included in this booklet were personally hiked by the writer during the 1976–1978 season. In checking out these areas, I found that many of them were hardly used at all and, at times, I was the only person on the trail. Perhaps a knowledge of other areas for hiking will help to decrease the number of people currently found on such popular trails as the Mesa Trail.

Since there are already some good trail guides available for hiking around East Portal, Fourth of July Campground, Brainard Lake, and Rocky Mountain Park, trails in these areas will not be included.

The aerial photos included in the booklet were taken by the writer from a private plane. I have found that sometimes it is difficult to visualize the area to be hiked from just looking at a topographical map; flying over the same area gives a much broader perspective.

Since this is a hiking booklet, no technical climbs will be included. The Boulder Public Library does have some good books available describing various rock climbs in the area.

There are some steeper climbs described in the booklet, such as to Mallory's Cave and up Fern Canyon, but none of these will require the use of technical equipment. However, you might find that "all fours" can be helpful at times.

Footwear is an important consideration on some of the steeper hikes, and particularly along the trails in the high country. Hiking boots offer better support than tennis shoes as well as providing protection from water.

Experience has shown that the "layering" method of dressing can be quite helpful. If the hiker begins with as much cotton next to the skin as possible, the hike will be much more comfortable.

Since the majority of the trails have little or no water available, the hiker would be well advised to carry a canteen, particularly during the hotter months.

Many of the hikes may be made as single hikes, or may be combined with other trails, making circular trips out of them. These trips are suggested in the booklet.

The question of timing for a particular hike is an individual matter. As a rule of thumb, it is better to allow too much time than to run the risk of having to grope your way back in the dark.

Acknowledgements

Special thanks go to Betty Reeves, Betty Lane, Buell Hamilton, Linda Light Bump of the Boulder County Open Space, Ralph Schell of Jefferson County Open Space, Brian Peck and Ann Wickman of the Boulder Mountain Parks, and to Ralph Johnson of the U.S. Forest Service for their assistance in finding new trails. I am also grateful to John and Adele Parmakian and Ray De Haan for looking over the original manuscript. Special thanks go to Warren De Haan for providing his services as a pilot to enable me to get the aerial shots.

Happy hiking!

October 1983:

Thanks to Rich Smith and Laurie Schwartz, Boulder park rangers, who took time to up-date me on the newest trails in the Boulder Mountain Parks and Open Space.

The Joy of Hiking
by
Vici De Haan

People often ask me why
I climb those mountains to the sky.
I would only reply:
    Have you ever
Walked through woods so deep and dark,
Along rushing streams cold and white,
Through fragrant meadows lush with flowers,
Up peaks with views unsurpassed
Or listened to the wind rustling through the trees
Or felt on your face the warmth of the sun
Or watched fluffy clouds that billow and float
Or smelled the forest after a rain
Or seen a deer bounding with alarm
Or flushed a ptarmigan that thought it was a rock
Or sat beside a mountain lake for lunch
Or shared your meal with a bumblebee
                  a camp robber
                  a chipmunk
                  a marmot
And been at total peace within your soul?
Then perhaps you too have known
The utter joy that a hike can bring.
    Happy hiking!

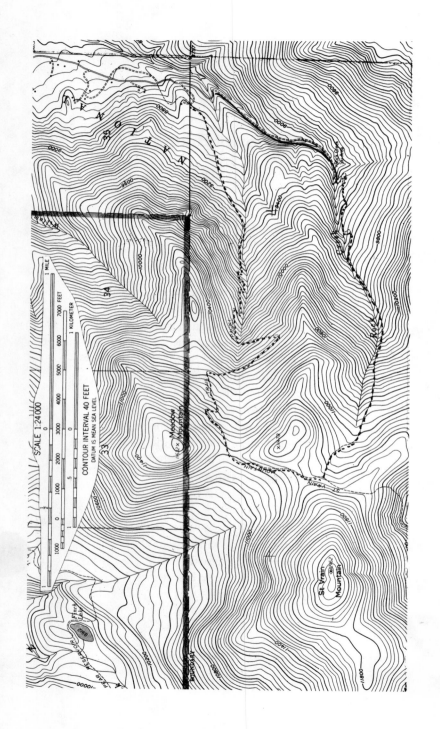

Allenspark Area

Meadow Mountain

St. Vrain Mountain

To reach these mountains, take Highway 36 to Lyons. From Lyons, take Highway 7 to Allenspark (20 miles). Turn left at the sign that indicates the Allenspark business area. Drive through Ferncliff and, after approximately 5 more miles, you will reach a dirt road heading south. The road has many signs on it, including two Ski Road signs. Turn left here and keep to the left at the next fork. After 1.8 miles, you reach another fork for the Meadow Mountain Trail. After .6 mile, you will reach a parking area for the trail. The signed trail goes through a beautiful forest to the southwest, and continues above timberline to below the summit of Meadow Mountain (11,630 feet). The trail doesn't take you to the top of the mountain itself, but since you are so high, you should have no difficulty selecting a good route up.

At timberline on the Meadow Mountain Trail

1

Allenspark: Once above timberline, beautiful
relics of trees are visible on the skyline.

To climb St. Vrain Mountain on the same day, return to the
trailhead used to climb Meadow Mountain and follow it over to
St. Vrain. Again you will have to choose your own route to the
top. St. Vrain is 12,162 feet high.

Distance to Meadow Mountain: 4 miles one way
Elevation gain: 2,800 feet
Distance to St. Vrain: 5½ miles one way
Additional elevation gain: 532 feet

Another option for climbing these peaks is to take the Rock
Creek Ski Road to the camping area. From here, if you have a
four-wheel-drive vehicle, you can go in a short distance before
leaving your car. Intercept the St. Vrain Glacier Trail and proceed from this trail to the summit of each peak as before.

Sunshine Canyon

Bald Mountain Scenic Area

Bald Mountain is an area which is used quite frequently by the Boulder Mountain Park rangers who offer nature hikes in the area. To reach Bald Mountain, go up Sunshine Canyon 4.3 miles west of Memorial Hospital. Bald Mountain is on the south side of the road. The trail is very well marked, climbing about 200 feet.

Total round trip: .5 mile

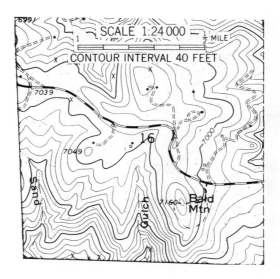

Bald Mountain: Sign at the entrance

Old wooden chute once used for loading
cattle around 1918. (Bald Mountain)

Betasso Preserve

Bummer's Rock

Canyon Trail

Bummer's Rock: The Betasso Preserve consists of 713 acres of forested land complete with some old mining equipment that might be of interest to mining buffs.

To reach the area, drive up Boulder Canyon to the Sugarloaf turn-off. Turn right and continue 1.3 miles, watching for the City of Boulder Water Treatment Plant sign. Turn right at the sign and go .4 mile to the Betasso Preserve.

To go to Bummer's Rock, don't turn into the area marked for the preserve, but stay on the main road for .1 mile. Watch for the concrete pad on the left-hand side of the road. A parking area is available directly opposite here with the unmarked trail to the rock which heads off to the south. It climbs through a beautiful pine forest and ends on some rocks that are fun to climb. The hiker also gets a good overlook of the canyons surrounding the preserve.

Distance: .5 mile
Elevation gained: 270 feet

Mining equipment found on Betasso Preserve

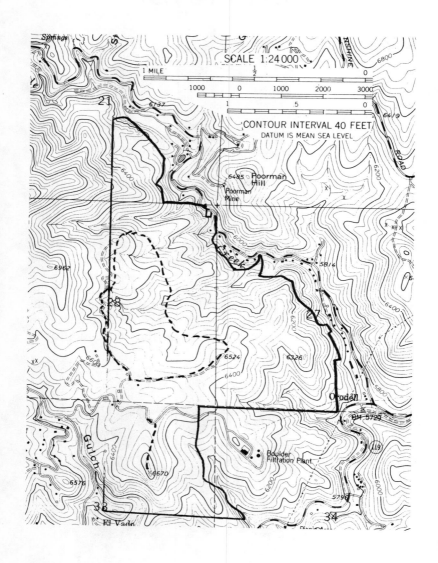

SCALE 1:24 000

CONTOUR INTERVAL 40 FEET
DATUM IS MEAN SEA LEVEL

6

Bummer's Rock

Old out-buildings near western end of Canyon Trail
at Betasso

Canyon Trail: For a longer hike, turn into the preserve and drive in .4 mile. Park by the side road where a log has been placed across two posts.

Walk along this road, heading east and then curving to the north. Just before this road loops back to the west, watch for another trail heading downhill to the east. You'll pass through a formerly gated area with the old iron gate propped open.

The trail drops steadily down for about 400 feet through a dense forest. Once at the bottom of the hill, you cross over a stream via a newly installed wooden bridge. From here, the ascent brings the hiker contouring around to the north and then west. The trail then joins a road going south. This road will bring you back to the fenced property. Follow the road going southeast and go through the gate. Stay on the road going east to return to your car.

Round trip: approximately 2.5 miles
Elevation lost and regained: approximately 400 feet

Eastern end of Canyon Trail

Boulder Mountain Parks

The trails in the Boulder foothills offer a great variety of hiking possibilities. Beginning with the easy hikes such as the Mesa Trail, the area also includes some very steep areas such as Mallory's Cave and Fern Canyon.

The trails in the park are clearly marked with color-coded circles. The color on the top of the circle indicates the difficulty of the hike. Green indicates an easy hike; yellow, a more difficult one; and red, the most difficult. Each trail then has its own color code as well, and this color is shown on the bottom of the circle.

Although the area also contains many good technical climbs, these will not be included.

The animal life in the park is quite diverse. If lucky, you may run across the large herd of deer that roam the mesa around NCAR, or see a fox just at dusk. There are many Abert squirrels

Sign guide for Boulder Mountain Parks trails

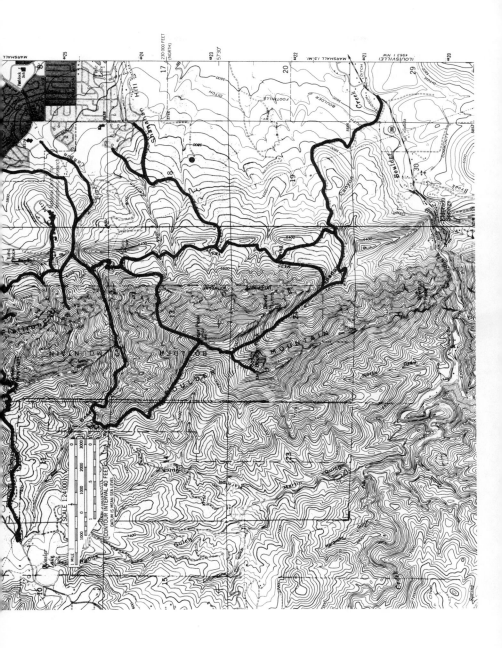

11

in the forests, as well as many jays that let you know they are around. There are also marmot to be found, near the National Bureau of Standards as well as on the southern end of the Mesa Trail.

The flowers along these trails are quite beautiful. The area offers a wide variety of blooms throughout the summer, making a hike along trails such as the Mesa Trail a real delight.

MESA TRAIL

Have you taken a walk through geological history lately? This can be done very easily by taking the Mesa Trail from Chautauqua to Eldorado Springs. The rock you see along this hike is the result of erosion from the ancestral Rockies which were located west of Boulder. The deposits have hardened into the sandstone which you see all about you.

The beginning of the southern end of the trail is often more exposed to the sun and therefore much hotter than the northern end, and so many hikers prefer to start at the northern end, which begins just below the Bluebell Canyon Shelter House. However, if the group is large enough, you might wish to consider exchanging car keys with a group beginning at either end.

The NCAR Service Road comes up from the lower left, below NCAR. Bear Creek runs along the left side of the road, after coming down the center of Bear Canyon visible in the upper right hand side of the aerial.

Looking southward along the Flatirons. Green Mountain is on the right. Bear Mountain and South Boulder Peak are further to the left.

The trail leaving Chautauqua passes through a beautiful forest of ponderosa pine. There are a few Abert squirrels in these woods. They may easily be identified by their black or gray color, and pointed, tufted ears. The forest is also the home for many Stellar jays which often screech at intruders.

About a mile from the start of the trail, the hiker has a good viewing point of the familiar Flatirons as well as of the old Woods-Bergheim rock quarry. A short distance further to the south, you'll pass a small stone cabin off to the west of you. This cabin is located on a half acre of private land that is surrounded by the city-owned land. It belongs to one of the original Boulder homesteaders and is sometimes rented out during the winter. It should be cheap housing since it offers no gas, electricity, or running water. The trail drops from here to cross Skunk Creek, then climbs to the meadow just west of NCAR. The spring and summer flowers along this meadow are quite spectacular.

Upon reaching the road, follow it to the west for a short distance, then turn south and cross Bear Creek. The road continues uphill to the south for a short distance before turning west and then south again. Just below the microwave tower, the trail leaves the road to go south through more woods and to cross more meadows.

Upon reaching the road, turn left to go to the southern end of the Mesa Trail back to the trailhead north of Eldorado Springs. If you follow this road to the right, you will come to the mouth of Shadow Canyon.

As you head southeast down the road, watch behind you for the rock formations called the Matron and the Maiden, often climbed by technical rock climbers. The cabin you pass part way down the road and off to the south of you was built in 1903 by one of the Dunn's workers in exchange for his room and board in their household. The stone was carried to the site by yoke of oxen and a cart.

As you approach Eldorado Springs, you get a good look at the Maiden and Devil's Thumb, both favorites for rock climbers.

Just before the end of the trail, watch for the marmots which often sun on the rocks, giving themselves away with their shrill cries.

The stone house, known as the Dunn Cabin, located at the very end of the trailhead was built in 1874–5 by John Debacker. He was one of the first families to homestead along South Boulder Creek during the 1860's. He raised chickens and cattle on the land. The Dunns bought the house in 1901 and lived there until 1953. The house, now padlocked, has one room downstairs and two upstairs, and is used by the Boulder Parks Department for storage purposes.

Distance one way: 6 miles
Elevation gain: 600 feet

Green
Red

Accesses to the Mesa Trail

There are numerous ways in which the hiker can get onto the Mesa Trail without always having to begin at either of its ends.
1. Begin at Chautauqua (northern access).
2. Begin at the southern end located off Highway 398 just outside of Eldorado Springs, 1.6 miles west of Highway 93 (Rocky Flats Road).

3 Loop Hikes from Eldorado Springs:
a. Middle Trail: Besides the Mesa Trail, you can follow a short spur for 1.25 miles up to join the Mesa Trail. This trail begins from behind the Dunn Cabin.

Walk around the north side of the cabin and watch for a narrower dirt road left of the one used for the Mesa Trail, which also heads to the west. This road passes through an old rock fence and continues to climb alongside a small creek up a very scenic draw. This trail eventually meets the Mesa Trail a short distance below the second cabin.

To make a loop hike, turn right and follow the road used by the Mesa Trail back down to the trailhead's beginning.

Loop distance: approximately 2.5 miles

b. Towhee Trail: Another trail to try behind the Dunn Cabin is the Towhee Trail, so named for the towhee birds in the area. Take the trail going to the south behind the house. After passing through the old stone fence, a faint spur takes off to the west. This trail can be seen climbing on the south side of the ridge with the power lines crossing it. The trail follows the draw on the other side of the Middle Trail, and climbs a hill before dropping back down to also join the Mesa Trail below the middle cabin.

c. Star Draw Trail: Another loop hike in this same area is to follow the Mesa Trail up to the first fork where a sign indicates that you can either stay left to go to Shadow Canyon or go to the right to stay on the Mesa Trail.

Stay to the right and continue to hike uphill to the west to the next intersection. Turn left to come to where the trail continues south to come to Shadow Canyon.

Upon reaching the Stockton cabin and the trail going up Shadow Canyon, turn left to go back down the Mesa Trail road which will lead you back to your starting point.

Loop distance: approximately 4.5 miles

3. Park at 17th and King (just off Baseline Road). The trail heads west from here over the ridge and then southwest until meeting the Mesa Trail.

Distance to the Mesa Trail: 1 mile

4. Shanahan and Greenslope Trails: This one is located in South Boulder. One starting point is located at the intersection of Lehigh and Lafayette Streets. To reach this intersection, take Table Mesa Drive west to Lehigh. Turn south on Lehigh and follow this street about one mile to where it meets Lafayette. An unmarked trail goes along the east side of the last house on the right side of the street as you crest Lehigh and intersect Lafayette. This path swings around to the right of the house and heads southwest towards a fence marking the greenbelt.

Cross the fence and continue west to reach the Shanahan Trail. After 1.6 miles, it joins the Mesa Trail.

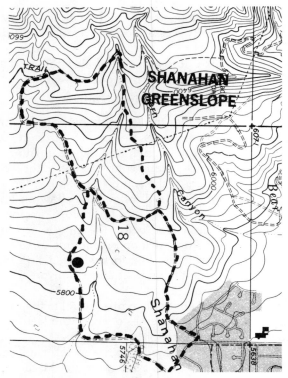

Another access to Shanahan Trail begins from Hardscrabble, 1 block east of the Lafayette/Lehigh intersection. Turn right on Hardscrabble, heading south and go to the end of the street to reach an established trailhead for Shanahan Trail.

Where the trail forks to the left after a few hundred yards, the left road goes .5 mile to a water tank. Instead, turn right and climb through a beautiful forested area. The trail forks once again about half way up. If you stay left, you'll continue on the Shanahan Trail which climbs up to join the Mesa Trail.

If you stay to the right, going around the information post, you'll also continue to climb up a fire road to the Mesa Trail, meeting it a short distance north of where the Shanahan Trail comes in.

To make a loop hike in the area, stay to the right at both lower intersections and climb up to the Mesa Trail. Then turn left onto the Mesa Trail and hike south a short distance to the Shanahan Trail. Turn east down the Shanahan Trail to return to your starting point.

16

Round trip: approximately 3.5 miles
Distance: 1.6 miles
Elevation gain: 640 feet

Green

Pink/
Yellow

Another starting point for this same trail is from the Devil's Thumb Subdivision at the intersection of View Point and Briarwood Streets. Go west into the cul de sac to park and hike through the gate, going southwest. A short distance after climbing the hill, this path will intersect the Shanahan Trail.

5. National Center for Atmospheric Research (NCAR)—two accesses

a. Park on Stony Hill Road, which is reached by following Table Mesa Drive west to Lehigh. Turn south on Lehigh for one block, then west onto Bear Mountain Drive. Turn west again onto Stony Hill Road. Park in the cul de sac at the end of this road and look for the trail which heads northwest. It crosses Bear Creek after a short distance and then links up with the NCAR Service Road. After about one mile, this road intersects the Mesa Trail which comes in from the north.

b. Park at the NCAR parking lot. This can be reached by taking Table Mesa Drive west to NCAR. Walk west beyond the buildings, going around on the north side, watching for the path which heads west. From here drop down and then climb one ridge before reaching the Mesa Trail.

Distance: .5 mile
Elevation gain: 80 feet

Green

Rust/Lt.
Green

6. Enchanted Mesa Trail: This trail, now widened into a fire road, is located near 12th and Mariposa where the road then swings behind the Chautauqua Theater. Park near the barrier and follow the road up to the city reservoir. The trail continues west from there, intersecting the Mesa Trail after 1.2 miles.

Elevation gain: 400 feet

Green

White/
Brown

7. McClintock Nature Trail: This trail starts at the west end of Mariposa and swings around east, staying below the Chautauqua Theater. The trail climbs gently up, crossing a small stream, to intersect the road leading to the Enchanted Mesa Trail. After crossing the road, it continues steeply up in a southerly direction

to where it meets the Mesa Trail. It has some good markers describing some of the natural features of the area.

Distance: .7 mile
Elevation gain: 400 feet

8. Bluebell-Baird Trail: Begin at Baird parking lot reached by driving west up Baseline Road to the base of Flagstaff Mountain. After crossing the stone bridge, turn left and drive west on a dirt road to a parking area. If you park facing south, you'll be facing the trailhead which crosses a small wooden bridge. At first you'll hike to the east and then to the south on your way to the Bluebell Shelter House.

Distance: .8 mile
Elevation gain: 300 feet

This trail may also be reached by taking the Chautauqua Trail located at the bottom of Bluebell Canyon Road. This beautiful mountain meadow walk goes southwest for .6 mile, climbing 280 feet to where it joins the Bluebell-Baird Trail.

To reach the Mesa Trail, go to the north of the shelter house and head downhill to the east. Where the road turns north, watch for a chain across the northern entrance to the Mesa Trail.

This trail can also be reached by hiking up the Bluebell Canyon Road, which has now been closed to vehicular traffic. Stay to the right at the fork and continue on to the picnic shelter. The trail begins off to your right and is marked.

Total distance from beginning of Bluebell-Baird Trail to Mesa Trail: 1.5 miles

Baird

Chautauqua

9. Table Mesa Drive: two accesses.

Skunk Creek Access: Skunk Creek Canyon was formed from the glacial runoff from millions of years ago and contains soil and boulders deposited by a river. The start of the trail by the pumphouse is an alluvial fan.

18

Your hike begins through Lyons sandstone. As you climb up, you can see Echo Rocks at the back of the NCAR Mesa. These rocks are formed of Dakota sandstone. As you proceed further up, you climb through the remnants of the Morrison and Lykins Formations.

To reach Skunk Creek Canyon, follow Table Mesa Drive west until you reach the end of the housing development. Watch for a bike trail off to the north side of the road. The bike trail is paved, and after a short distance, it joins a dirt road. Stay with this dirt road and south of the houses, heading to the west. When you reach the pumphouse at the end of the road, continue straight ahead to the west, crossing Skunk Creek. Watch out for poison ivy on the west side of the creek. At the fork just beyond the creek, keep to the left and climb in a westerly direction to join the Mesa Trail.

Distance: 1.5 miles

Another access begins at the same place as above. Instead of taking the north bikepath, take the dirt road which heads south. This road goes on the west side of the houses for approximately 1 mile before turning southwest on the north side of the power station. After approximately another half mile, this trail links up with the NCAR Service Road approximately one mile below the Mesa Trail.

Distance to Mesa Trail: 2½ miles

Mesa Trail Circle Trip

For a round trip in the southern part of town, take Table Mesa Drive west to Lehigh. Turn south for one block and then turn west onto Bear Mountain Drive. Proceed west to Stony Hill Road. Park in the cul de sac and pick up the trail going northwest. Cross Bear Creek and pick up the NCAR Service Road. Follow this road west, then south as it crosses Bear Creek again. Stay with the road as it bends west and then south until you are just below the microwave tower. Distance this far is approximately 2 miles.

Pick up the Mesa Trail and continue to hike for approximately one mile, watching for the Shanahan Trail which intersects the Mesa Trail from the east. Now to complete the trip, follow the Shanahan Trail back out.

The best access to your car is to watch for where the trail is just about out of the trees and you can just begin to see the houses in the Devil's Thumb Subdivision. There is a trail here that heads northeast from the Shanahan Trail which will drop you down to the intersection of Briarwood and View Point Road. Follow View Point Road to Bear Mountain Drive and then on to Stony Hill to retrieve your car.

Should you miss this cutoff to Devil's Thumb, the Shanahan Trail continues out to Hardscrabble. To return to your car, hike north out Hardscrabble to Lehigh. Turn left and follow Lehigh to Briarwood. Turn left and follow Briarwood to View Point Road. Turn right. This road will now lead you back to Stoney Hill Road.

Total round trip: approximately 5 miles

Chautauqua Round Trips

1. Go up Chautauqua Trail from the bottom of the meadow in Chautauqua Park to where it intersects the Bluebell-Baird Trail. Proceed along this trail until reaching the Bluebell Shelter House. From here, stay to the left of the shelter and head first north and then west along the paved road to the Mesa Trail's northern entrance.

To head back to your parked car at Chautauqua, either follow the Mesa Trail to the McClintock Nature Trail and down, or continue farther along the Mesa Trail until reaching the Enchanted Mesa Trail. This trail ends behind the Chautauqua Theater. Continue north along the paved road until past the theater, then cross to the west across the grass to retrieve your car.

2. Park in Baird Park. Take the Amphitheater Trail for a very short distance, watching for a fork off to the left, heading east. Now you are on the Bluebell-Baird Trail which will take you to the Bluebell Shelter House. From here you can take the road back down to the bottom of Chautauqua and then pick up the trail that crosses to the west along the bottom of the meadow, taking you back to your car in Baird Park.

Total distance: approximately 5.3 miles

Mallory's Cave

Cave Hikes from the Mesa Trail: Mallory Cave, Bear Cave, and Harmon Cave

Mallory Cave: This is the largest cave known in the park, and is one of the most difficult hikes. A fast access to the trail leading to the cave would be to take the NCAR Trail west of the NCAR buildings to where it intersects the Mesa Trail. Turn south for a short distance, watching for the Mallory Cave trailhead marker off to the west.

The climb to the cave from the trail involves a good rock scramble of about 30 feet, but this trail is one which affords a tremendous view of the Flatirons and their uplifted rocks as well as a good overlook of the city.

Distance one way: .4 mile
Elevation gain: 700 feet

Red

Blue

Bear Cave: This is a very small cave, but for those who enjoy visiting caves, it might be worth the time to find it.

Go up the Bear Canyon Trail which is reached by first going west on the NCAR Trail and turning south onto the Mesa Trail. Continue to follow the Mesa Trail as it joins the NCAR Service Road. The road heads west, then south crossing Bear Creek, and then west once again. Upon reaching the top of the next hill and

Large rock slab located
beside the trail to Bear Cave

Bear Cave is on the right

22

heading west, watch for the large power antennna and a trail marker for Bear Canyon.

Follow this trail west for about a quarter of a mile. Watch for a large rock slab and a place along the hillside to your right were others have scrambled down to the creek. It's marked with three steel posts in the ground below the trail. After the trail descends to cross Bear Creek, it then involves a steep scramble up the hillside north of the creek for about .25 mile. The cave does bear a faint resemblance to a small black bear.

Harmon Cave: This is a medium-sized cave located just off the Mesa Trail. To reach it, take the Mesa Trail to its intersection with Bear Canyon, as described in the Bear Cave hike. Continue uphill to the south for a short distance after passing the Bear Canyon Trail, watching carefully on the upper hillside for an un-marked trail heading off to your right to the west.

When you spot the faint trail, you'll see that the bank you'll have to scramble up to reach it is quite steep, so you may wish to proceed further up the road a short distance to climb up the bank and then return to the trail.

Harmon Cave

The trail climbs steeply between two talus slopes of rock for approximately .25 mile. The cave is clearly visible off to your right as you come out into a small meadow. Boulder Mountain Parks would probably rate this spur as one of their most difficult hikes since it's quite steep.

Distance from Mesa Trail: approximately .5 mile

Royal Arch

This is truly a "heads up" hike, because the trail markers have been posted along the trees, and when climbing the steeper section, your eyes will more than likely be down.

The hike begins south of the Bluebell Shelter House near the picnic table that is just off the road.

The trail itself is steep, ranked as an intermediate hike. It climbs first on the west side and then on the east side of Bluebell Canyon. Upon reaching the saddle, you get two good views. One looks out over Boulder to the southeast, and by going a few feet to the right of the rocks on the saddle, you get a good look at the arch itself.

Royal Arch signpost

Looking south through the
arch

Watch for a sign posted by the Colorado Mountain Club at
the saddle, for it is easy to get off onto a false trail here. From the
saddle, the trail descends about 80 feet before climbing back up
between some gateway rocks. The last stretch climbs south until
you arrive at the natural sandstone arch affording the climber a
well-won view of Boulder and another of the Flatirons.

Distance: 5 mile round trip
Elevation gain: 1,200 feet

Yellow

Blue

Bear Peak Via Bear Canyon and Bear Canyon West Ridge

Bear Peak, located on the southern side of the Flatirons, is a very beautiful climb. Once on top, the climber can truly see the full effect of the beetles that effectively killed the majority of the trees on the western slopes.

To begin the hike, park at NCAR. Take the NCAR Trail until it meets the Mesa Trail, where you will continue south to the intersection of the Mesa Trail and the NCAR Service Road. This road goes west a short distance, then turns south to cross Bear Creek. It then climbs uphill to the south before turning west again. At the top of this hill, watch for the power substation located on a trail which heads to the west, while the road portion of the Mesa Trail continues to the south. The Bear Canyon trailhead is by this power station and has been marked by a Boulder Mountain Parks signpost.

Follow this trail west for 1.5 miles, climbing 900 feet and crossing Bear Creek several times. Just before reaching the West Ridge Trail, you will climb up a steep hill. Once you drop down the other side of this hill, watch for the trail which crosses Bear Creek once more and heads to the south. Follow the Bear Peak West Ridge Trail until reaching the west ridge of the peak. From here, head southeast to where you will have a good scramble through the talus and boulders found just below the summit.

Distance one way to the summit: 3.2 miles
Elevation gain: approximately 2,200 feet

Bear Canyon's beginning as it leaves the NCAR Road

Uptilted sandstone rocks
along Bear Canyon

One of the many good views
of the Flatirons as seen from
the Bear Canyon Trail

Bear Peak Via Fern Canyon

This is one of the steepest accesses to the peak, and is often used as a descent. The Boulder Parks Department rates this as one of their most difficult hikes.

To reach the Fern Canyon trailhead, you can take the NCAR Service Road. To reach it, drive west on Table Mesa Drive to Lehigh. Turn south for one block on Lehigh, and then west onto Bear Mountain Drive. Follow this street to Stony Hill Road. Park in the cul de sac at the end of this road and watch for the trail which heads northwest. It crosses Bear Creek after a short distance and then links up with the NCAR Service Road.

Follow the service road to the west, turning south to cross Bear Creek. Stay with the road as it turns south; just below the microwave tower, you should begin watching for the trail sign posted on the right, a short distance below the Mesa Trail turn off.

This trail is not only steep, but difficult to follow since the mountain is now full of false trails going everywhere. If you get off the trail while in the canyon, you can find yourself in for some rough rock scrambling.

At first the trail climbs southwest, then south before turning to the west. Just below the large rock slab on the north side of the trail, you will find the many ferns that gave this trail its name.

One of Bear Canyon's
steeper sections

Fern Canyon Trail just
before the going gets tough

A rock slab visible along
Fern Canyon

Near the large slab, watch for Fern Spring, marked by an old metal marker on a tree. Stay with the trail heading straight up and to the west.

Once you reach the saddle located between Nebel Horn and Bear Peak, climb to the southwest, staying on the ridge. This leads you into some talus which makes the climbing of Bear Peak a good challenge, but one which has its own rewards.

Fern Canyon distance one way: 1.3 miles
Distance from NCAR Road to summit: 3.5 miles
Elevation gain via Fern to summit: 2,100 feet

Red
Light
Green

South Boulder Peak Via Shadow Canyon

The easiest access for this peak, joined to Bear Peak by a saddle, is from the southern entrance to the Mesa Trail off Highway 398. Travel up the trail for two miles, following it to the Stockton cabin. This cabin is located at the end of the road.

Cross the small pond to the west of the cabin and pick up the Shadow Canyon Trail which heads straight up in a westerly direction. On the way, you will pass two favorites for rock climbers: Devil's Thumb and the Maiden.

DeBacker cabin along the southern end of the Mesa Trail

Stockton cabin just
below the beginning
of Shadow Canyon

Shadow Canyon signpost

31

Once you reach the shoulder, you can decide which peak you wish to climb first. In order to climb South Boulder Peak, watch for a faint trail going to the southwest which ends up in some very large boulders. From here you have a scramble to the summit and a tremendous view of the mountains to the west.

South Boulder Peak is 8,550 feet.
Distance one way: 3.6 miles
Elevation gain: 2,700 feet

Yellow
Lt. Green/
Orange

Shadow

Yellow
Gray/Rust

So. Boulder Peak

View of the Maiden, clearly visible from Shadow Canyon

Bear Peak

There is no marked trail for climbing Bear Peak. From this same shoulder at the top of Shadow Canyon, turn to the north. Be sure to stay on about the same elevation but on the west side of the mountain. You will wind through the forest to a talus slope. At this point you should also meet the Bear Peak West Ridge Trail. Take this trail to the summit.

Bear Peak is 8,461 feet.
Distance one way: 3.7 miles from Mesa Trail
Elevation gain: 2,700 feet

Yellow

Black/ Purple

Bear Canyon, West Ridge

South Boulder or Bear Peak Round Trip

A two-car shuttle is necessary for this one. Leave one car in the NCAR parking lot. Drive the other car to begin from the southern entrance to the Mesa Trail, and take the Shadow Canyon Trail up to either peak. To climb both in one day, first climb South Boulder Peak, and then drop back to the saddle and climb up Bear Peak.

There are now two options for returning to your car. You can pick up the Bear Peak West Ridge Trail which will take you back to Bear Canyon. From there, pick up the Mesa Trail and follow it back to the NCAR Trail and back to your car.

Another possibility is to leave Bear Peak via the Fern Canyon Trail. This trail also brings you to the Mesa Trail just a short distance south of Bear Canyon. The return to your car is then about the same as for the first option.

Distance up South Boulder-Bear Peak via Shadow Canyon and returning via Bear Peak West Ridge: approximately 9 miles
Distance up South Boulder-Bear Peak via Shadow Canyon and returning via Fern Canyon: approximately 7 miles

South Boulder Peak-Bear Peak: Shadow Canyon splits the two peaks on the left-hand side of the picture. Fern Canyon, with its rock slab on the north side of the trail, is also visible.

Flagstaff Road is visible climbing the mountain on the left side of the photo. Boulder Canyon winds its way up in the foreground.

Flagstaff

Anyone traveling west on Baseline Road can see the flagpole that is on top of Flagstaff Mountain. In order to reach the summit on foot, drive over the stone bridge that is on Baseline Road as it turns north up Flagstaff. Right after crossing the bridge, watch for a dirt road which leads to Baird Park, and which is off to the west. Park at the intersection of Baird Park Road and Baseline Road, for the trailhead is off to the north of here.

The trail climbs steeply to the northwest before gradually leveling off to cross through some beautiful shrubs and flowers. Then the trail begins to climb steadily up to the first crossing of Flagstaff Road. You will cross this road four times, with each crossing marked by painted lines along the road. However, the last time you cross the road, you will need to walk to your right or to the east for a few hundred yards to get back onto the trail. It is located in a pull-out area on the northeast side of the road.

While you are on this last and steepest stretch, you can easily reach the flagpole by taking the last right-hand spur, or the Plains Overlook Trail, which leads you to the lookout. Otherwise, by continuing on with the Flagstaff Trail, you will once again reach Flagstaff Road near the overlook on top.

Once on the top of Flagstaff Road, you'll see a summit house to your right on the way to the amphitheater. The house has some natural displays inside. In 1983, the summit house was open weekends during the summer. You may wish to check with the

Flagpole on the summit of Flagstaff

Parks Department to see about its hours if you should want to look around. Hikers will also be pleased to know that they can find water in a nearby tank which is provided by the Boulder Mountain Parks. If you find that the tank is empty, please notify them so they can refill it.

Distance: 1.5 miles
Elevation gain: 1,050 feet

Yellow
White

Additional Flagstaff Mountain Trails

Boy Scout Trail and May's Point: One end of this trail begins at the northeast corner of the Sunrise Circle Amphitheater located on the top of Flagstaff and off to the south of the overlook parking area. The trail comes out by the picnic area on the northwest side of the mountain.

Boy Scout Trail as it comes off Flagstaff

To pick up the trail from the picnic area, take the road from the summit to the northwest for a short distance. Park by the picnic table and take the trail going downhill to the west. After approximately .3 mile, there is another path that takes off to the west to May's Point, but which is unmarked. The Boy Scout Trail continues to the east at this intersection, ending up at the amphitheater. There are some good overlooks of Mount Sanitas along this walk.

Distance one way: .6 mile
Elevation gain: 80 feet

Boy Scout

May's Point

Tenderfoot Trail: Begin at Realization Point and the picnic area on the northeast side of the road. Realization Point is located about three-fourths of the way to the top of Flagstaff Mountain where Flagstaff Road turns back to the east and the Kossler Lake Road continues to the west. The trail heads north for about a mile before intersecting an old road going to the west. After going down for a short distance, this old road heads uphill quite steeply. From the top of this hill, the road continues off to the south. However, since this road leads to a road on private property, permission should be obtained before taking it. The road ends up in Boulder Canyon.

Distance one way: 1.5 miles
Elevation gain: 1,000 feet

Tenderfoot

Ute Trail: This trail has two possible starting points along the top of Flagstaff. The southern trail may be picked up by crossing Flagstaff Road and turning to the southwest after you climb the stone stairs by an old well. The trail heads downhill on the side of the mountain and ends up at Realization Point.

The northwest trail begins from the Range View Trail which starts behind the shelter house on Flagstaff, and it is well marked at its beginning with many stones. Watch for the Ute Trail; it

Tenderfoot Trail junction with Range View at
Realization Point

Tenderfoot Trail

Ute Trail as it climbs on the south side of Flagstaff

takes off to the right and goes downhill steeply. After a short distance, it meets the Boy Scout Trail.

Distance one way on southwest trail: .5 mile
Elevation gain from Realization Point: 160 feet

Green
Green

Plains Overlook: This short trail may be picked up in two places. First, you can begin at the Sunrise Circle Amphitheater on the south side of the lookout on Flagstaff Mountain. Here you take the first right-hand trail that goes west.

The other access is from the Flagstaff Trail, just a short distance before it meets Flagstaff Road. The Plains Overlook trail takes off to the northeast and gives a beautiful overlook of the plains to the east.

Distance one way: .3 mile
Elevation gain: 40 feet

Green
Yellow

Range View Trail: This is another trail on the top of Flagstaff. To find its beginning, proceed west of the shelter house on the northwest side of the mountain. The trail is well marked with stones, and winds around the shoulder of Flagstaff, affording a tremendous view of the flat top of Long's Peak off to the northwest, of Audubon with its giant "crater" left behind by a glacier, and of Arapaho Glacier, one of Boulder's sources of water. The trail ends up at Realization Point.

Distance one way: .5 mile
Elevation gain: 160 feet

Yellow
Red

Range View Trail offers good views of the mountains to the west

Gregory Canyon: When hiking this trail uphill, and crossing some of the rocky areas, it is hard to imagine that this was once part of the old stage road going to Magnolia. The trail begins at the west end of the Baird parking lot. Head west through some beautiful shrubbery, particularly during the fall, and climb uphill until you meet the road that continues west to the Green Mountain Lodge.

Distance one way: 1.2 mile
Elevation gain: 800 feet

Yellow
Sage
Green

Gregory Canyon's rocky trail was once an old stage road

Circle Trips on Flagstaff: To go up, take the Flagstaff Trail all the way to the road that comes up to the top. Then head northwest behind the shelter house to intercept the Range View Trail. This trail will take you to below the very top of Flagstaff, and circles the mountain, eventually dropping onto the west side of the mountain at Realization Point.

When you reach the picnic table at Realization Point, cross the road going to Kossler Lake and pick up the dirt road going downhill to the southwest. Stay to your right at the first switchback. This fire road will then go west, heading for the Green Mountain Shelter. At the next intersection, you leave the road to go downhill to the east until you come to the green tank. Here turn to the south, crossing the creek, and pick up the Gregory Canyon Trail which will return you to your car.

For a slight variation on this, stay with the Flagstaff Trail as for the above hike. Then, instead of picking up the Range View Trail, pick up the Ute Trail on the southwest side of Flagstaff and follow this trail down to Realization Point. Then once again pick up the Gregory Canyon Trail and continue back to your car.

Round trip: approximately 4 miles

Green Mountain

Green Mountain is one of those must hikes in the Boulder Parks. If lucky, the hiker might just be on top at the same time a glider decides to ride the winds that provide lift for it.

There are several routes that can be taken to the summit.

Gregory Canyon—Saddle Rock—H.L. Greenman: To reach the Gregory Canyon Trailhead which is located at the bottom of Flagstaff Mountain at Baird Park, drive into the Baird Park parking area located west of the bridge where Flagstaff Road turns north. Park here and head south of the Boulder Parks sign which is posted directly west of the parking lot. Cross over the bridge that takes you to the Saddle Rock/Amphitheater Trail. You climb south at first before turning west. The trail is 1.2 mile long and climbs 1,200 feet.

This trail will then continue to the southwest to connect with the H.L. Greenman Trail. This trail will take you to the summit of Green Mountain. The Greenman Trail is 1.5 miles long with an elevation gain of 1,500 feet.

Distance one way up Green Mountain: 3.2 miles
Elevation gain: 2,700 feet

Yellow	Yellow	Yellow	Yellow
Sage Green	Gray	Dark Blue	Pink
Gregory Canyon	Saddle Rock	Amphitheater	H. L. Greenman

One of Saddle Rock's less steep sections

Saddle Rock Trail at its intersection with
Greenman Trail

Amphitheater Trailhead

Amphitheater: a rock climber's favorite

Gregory Canyon — Ranger Trail: Another option is to take Gregory Canyon to the Green Mountain Shelter House. Then, instead of taking the H.L. Greenman Trail, continue to follow the Ranger Trail when it forks right until it intersects the Green Mountain West Ridge Trail which will take you to the summit.

Distance one way: 5.0 miles
Elevation gain: 2,850 feet

Yellow

Black

Ranger

Along the lower portion of the Ranger Trail, there is an interesting side trip that may be made to an old cabin. To get there, watch for a little-traveled trail a few hundred yards off to the left and just above the Green Mountain Shelter House.

Ranger Trail — Green Mountain West Ridge or H.L. Greenman (starting from Realization Point): A shorter hike up Green Mountain is to drive to the point on Flagstaff Road where this road turns east and Kossler Lake Road continues to the west. Park here and follow the fire road to the Green Mountain Shelter. Here you have the option of taking either the left fork up H.L. Greenman Trail to the top or remaining with the Ranger

Green Mountain Shelter

Trail to its intersection with the Green Mountain West Ridge Trail and then on to the summit.

Distance via Greenman Trail: 1.5 miles
Elevation gain: 1,500 feet
Distance via Ranger — Green Mountain West Ridge: 2.3 miles
Elevation gain: 1,450 feet

Yellow
Yellow

West Ridge

The views from the top of Green Mountain include some of the state's 14,000 foot peaks: Longs, Evans, and Bierstadt; as well as some peaks over 13,000 feet: Arapaho, Meeker, and Audubon. Watch for the stone cairn on the top of the mountain with its circular plaque that points out some of the various peaks along the Continental Divide. There is also a registration canister for hikers to sign which is located within this rock cairn.

Long Canyon

This is a beautifully wooded trail which can be reached from Realization Point. Begin on the fire road going southwest, passing the fire gate and keeping to the right when another branch of the road heads east. Continue to the Green Mountain Shelter House, where you go north around the house, crossing a bridge.

Long Canyon Trail as it leaves Flagstaff Road

Entrance to the Green Mountain West Ridge Trail

The trail then goes west from here. The trail comes out on the Kossler Lake Road. From here, the hiker can go up the road .4 of a mile and catch the Green Mountain West Ridge Trail to continue on to the summit of Green Mountain.

Distance one way: 2.5 miles
Elevation gain: 1,350 feet

Yellow
Dark Green

Long Canyon

For those willing to follow a trail that is rather faint but which offers a quiet woodsy hike, there is another trail which intersects the Long Canyon Trail and eventually winds its way through the woods until it also meets the Green Mountain West Ridge Trail without having to follow the Kossler Lake Road.

To find this trail, located at the western end of the Long Canyon Trail, and just before you walk out of the woods onto the road, bear to your left and watch for a trail heading west and then south. The trail contours around on the east side of the ridge before crossing over to the next ridge where the trail runs south, running into a fence. The West Ridge Green Mountain Trail can then be intercepted from here.

Green Mountain West Ridge

This is one of the quickest accesses to Green Mountain as well as being one of the shortest. To reach the trailhead, take Flagstaff Road up and continue past the turnoff to Flagstaff's summit, continuing west towards Kossler Lake. From 6th and Baseline, the trailhead is approximately 4.7 miles up the road, and is located on the south or left-hand side of the road. It is marked with a Boulder Parks trail sign. There is also a chain across the road which serves as the trailhead.

This trail is well marked by double yellow Boulder Parks signs on its lower portion. The upper part of the trail was recently (1983) vastly improved and is now quite easy to follow. As you near the top of the mountain, watch for some wild raspberries in late August.

Distance one way from Flagstaff Road: 1.5 miles
Elevation gain: 600 feet

Yellow
Yellow

One of the twin springs on Green Mountain

Marker at summit of Green Mountain

Green Mountain Circle Trips

1. Go up Gregory Canyon Trail to the Range View Trail. From here, intersect the Ranger Trail and then the Greenman Trail heading for Green Mountain's summit. Return via the Saddle Rock Trail. Note: watch for this trail off to your right after you come down the steepest section of the Greenman Trail. It's been marked by a Boulder Mountain Parks sign.

Round trip: approximately 5.7 miles

2. Go up Gregory Canyon to the Ranger Trail behind the Green Mountain Shelter House and stay with this trail until it meets with the Green Mountain West Ridge Trail. Return via the Greenman-Ranger and Gregory Canyon trails.

Total distance: approximately 5.8 miles

3. Begin at Realization Point. Go up Long Canyon to the right of the Green Mountain Shelter House. Follow the Kossler Lake Road for .4 of a mile, watching for the West Ridge of the Green Mountain Trail. Return via the Greenman Trail.

Distance: approximately 4.4 miles

North Boulder Trails

Mount Sanitas

Fire Road

Red Rocks

Aqueduct Trail

Centennial Park Round Trip

Mount Sanitas: The trailhead is located just west of Memorial Hospital at 4th and Mapleton in North Boulder. Proceed just behind the hospital for approximately ¼ mile and watch for the Knollwood Subdivision sign. The parking area for Mount Sanitas is north of this area on the north side of the road.

This is a steep climb with much loose rock, making the wearing of hiking boots advisable. Beginning from the parking area, head north for a short distance, watching for the trail going west and uphill. The trail is well marked; it goes to the south of the ridge, and then it heads northwesterly to the top. Upon reaching the summit, you will find a metal pole cemented onto one of the rocks. At this location, there are some good overlooks of both the city to the east as well as of the mountains to the west.

Distance one way: 1.2 miles
Elevation gain: 1,200 feet

Fire Road: This road is located directly west of Memorial Hospital on the north side of the road. This is a jogger's delight, since it climbs very gradually up to some rock quarries.

Go around the fire barrier to head north. After approximately ¾ mile, the first road turning left leads to a rock quarry. Continuing on the road to the north, the hiker will pass through a good-sized prairie dog colony. The road then bends to the west and climbs up to another rock quarry.

Distance one way to top rock quarry: approximately 1.5 miles
Elevation gain: 200 feet

Mt. Sanitas trail marker

Uptilted sandstone slabs along Sanitas

51

A twisted tree still stands along the Sanitas Trail

Much sandstone was once quarried from this area

One of the many prairie
dogs that live along the Fire
Road

Red Rocks Park: Centennial Foothills Park has some beautiful hikes available to both the rock scrambler and to anyone who just likes to get up onto a high piece of ground to look out over the city as well as towards the Continental Divide.

The access to the park is reached by driving west up Mapleton toward Memorial Hospital. From the intersection of Mapleton and 4th, the trailhead is located .3 of a mile west and on the left-hand side of the road. A parking area is located here.

Should you decide to do some rock scrambling, follow the trail going south and watch for another trail turning off to the east, going up to the uptilted rocks.

Red Rocks was where the first white settlers of Boulder established a camp on October 17, 1858. A story is told about a wagon that was attacked by a band of Indians who massacred the family aboard with the exception of a 13 year old girl. She escaped and hid in the rocks, but was found by one of the Indians and also shot with an arrow. Her initials are reportedly carved on the rocks near the site.

Distance: .5 mile one way
Elevation gain: 400 feet

Yellow

Orange/
Brown

Red Rocks Park: These
sandstone rocks have many
cracks and crevices and
even some small caves to
explore.

A rock scrambler looks for
another route at Red Rocks

Aqueduct Trail: If the hiker prefers something more challenging in distance, take the road as it heads to the south, and watch for a very steep climb off the west. Here the original ascent is quite steep, but once it levels out, the hiker has some very gentle, rolling hilltops to walk along. The trail that follows the ridge intersects the road just at the top of its steepest part, heading off to the northwest. If you happen to miss the trail, you can bushwhack west up to the first ridge and find it. The trail then leads across three other ridges with very little altitude gain or loss until it comes to an end on a ridge that is south of the Mount Sanitas ridge.

From here, the hiker can either follow the trail back down to the west or retrace original footsteps.

There is some beautiful smoky quartz as you go up the road, easily visible because the trail is quite steep and your head is usually down.

Distance: approximately 2 miles one way
Elevation gain: approximately 400 feet

Centennial Park Round Trip: Begin in Foothills Centennial Park. Take the trail heading·southwest along the Sunshine Canyon Road until you reach the end of an old barbed wire fence. Follow the fence uphill to catch the trail again. This trail gradually winds its way up to the top of a ridge. Once on top, take the fork to your left, heading east. This trail goes around the north side of the mountain, crossing the top of the ridge a couple of times. Whenever the trail seems to be dim, stay on the north side of the ridge and it will soon become apparent again.

Total round trip: approximately 3 miles

Eldora Ski Area Trails

Guinn Mountain

Bryan Mountain

Loop Hike

Guinn and Bryan Mountains: To reach the trailhead, take Boulder Canyon to Nederland and continue through Nederland on Highway 119 to the southwest. Turn north onto the Lake Eldora road after 1 mile. You will then reach a fork in the road after 1.5 miles. Here you take the left turn for Lake Eldora. The ski area is approximately 21 miles from Boulder.

Park in the ski lot only if you know that you can retrieve your car by 4:30, because the gate will be locked at that time. If in doubt about your return, you can park just outside the gate.

There are four possible routes up Bryan and Guinn Mountains:

1. The most direct route up Bryan Mountain is from the ski lodge. From here you can hike up the Cannonball ski run just west of the lodge. At the top of this hill, look for the ski-area road that continues off to the west, and after leaving the area, continues on to the shoulder of Bryan Mountain which is 10,796 feet. From this point, it is only a short distance to the summit.

Bryan is a good above-timberline hike which gives the hiker a good 360° view of the surrounding terrain.

Distance one way to Bryan: approximately 2½ miles
Elevation gain: 1,523 feet

To reach Guinn Mountain, continue along the old pipeline roadcut for another 1½ miles. Leave the road to hike to the summit of Guinn.

Distance from Lake Eldora one way: 4 miles
Additional elevation gain: 284 feet

2. Park in the southeast corner of the parking lot of the ski area. Going around the east side of the ticket booth, pick up the 17th Avenue ski-touring trail. After 1 mile, you reach an intersection with Dead Man's Gulch Trail. Turn west here and continue down the hill into Jenny Creek Meadow. Stay on the road

Lake Eldora Ski Area. Starting at the top left, you can see the pipeline road which leads to below Guinn and Bryan Mountains. Photo also shows the hiker why to avoid coming down the ski run in the back of the ski area.

Snow-covered stump in the winter along Jenny Creek

on the north side of the meadow, keeping Jenny Creek on your left. After approximately 3 miles, you will cross a tributary creek (which is often quite high in the early summer), and the road now begins to climb above Jenny Creek.

Turn right as the trail forks and now the trail becomes steeper. After about 1½ miles, you will come to a three-way intersection. Stay left and follow the red-flagged road. Once you reach the clearing on the shoulder of the mountain, you will see a metal building. To reach Guinn Mountain Hut, maintained by the Colorado Mountain Club, continue west another few hundred feet. The hut is located on the south side of Guinn Mountain.

To climb Guinn, it might be easiest to turn north at the metal building and pick up the old pipeline road. After a short distance, you can easily see the summit of the mountain (11,080 feet) off to the west, and you can make your own way up.

Distance: 5.2 miles one way
Elevation gain: 1,850 feet

3. To climb Guinn from the ski lodge, begin on the service road that is located southeast of the lodge and runs beside a small pond. This road curves back to the east toward the bunny

Guinn Mountain Hut in March

slope before gradually going up to the service road going out of the area. This pipeline road will take the hiker along the ridge between the two mountains.

To climb Bryan, bushwhack to the east. To climb Guinn Mountain, bushwhack up the mountain to the west.

4. Forest access to Jenny Creek and Guinn Mountain: Park in the lower lot by the ski ticket building. Then instead of taking the 17th Avenue touring trail to the east, stay to the west and climb the hill beside the Ho Hum chairlift.

Once on top of this hill, cross behind and south of the lift and follow the Foxtail ski trail until just below the steep hill or the Upper Bunnyfair ski trail.

Here watch for the forest-access signs as well as ski-touring signs. This access trail parallels the ski trail for a few hundred yards before taking off to the southwest and later to the west until it drops down the mountain ridge into Jenny Creek.

Once on the Jenny Creek trail, continue to Guinn Mountain as described above.

Loop Hike: For a loop, begin with the trail by the ticket office in the southeast part of the ski area, taking Jenny Creek up to Guinn Mountain. From there, continue along the pipeline road to Bryan Mountain. This road will then take you back into the ski area. At this point, be sure to continue along the road to the east, since the first ski run you come to will dump you onto the wrong side of the mountain from your car.

Round trip: approximately 9 miles

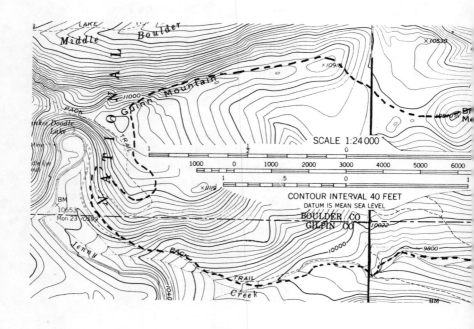

SCALE 1:24 000

CONTOUR INTERVAL 40 FEET
DATUM IS MEAN SEA LEVEL

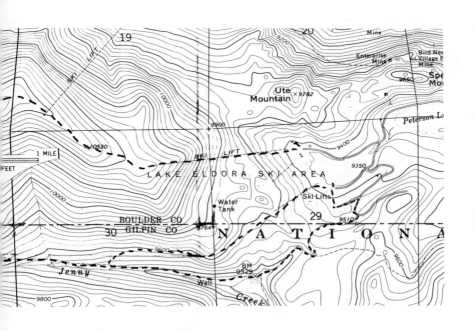

Town of Eldora

Eldorado Mountain

Mineral Mountain

Caribou Hill

Klondike Mountain

Spencer Mountain

Eldorado Mountain, Mineral Mountain, Caribou Hill, and Klondike Mountain: Have you ever come out of the woods at sunset just in time to watch the sun's rays color the blowing snow from the Continental Divide? If not, try hiking this trail just after the first snowfall in the high country.

The peaks may be climbed out of the town of Eldora, 24 miles west of Boulder. Take Highway 119 to Nederland, continuing through Nederland for one mile to the Lake Eldora turn-off. Stay to the right where the Lake Eldora Road turns left. The town of Eldora is approximately four miles from Highway 119.

Aerial shows the Lake Eldora Ski area in the upper left. To the right is the ridge of mountains including Eldorado, Mineral, and Caribou.

Trailer at the beginning of Eldorado Mountain

Upon reaching the town, go to the center to the street where the Log Cabin Grocery is on the northeast side. Turn right here, going north for two blocks, passing the Gold Miner Hotel off to the west. Turn right (east) for one more block and park here along the street. Walk north for one more block, watching for a large white trailer on the northeast side of the road, and turn to the east. This jeep road travels east, then turns west to cross just below Eldorado Mountain at 9,660 feet. The road then continues

Looking west from Eldorado Mountain Trail towards Lake Eldora Ski Area.

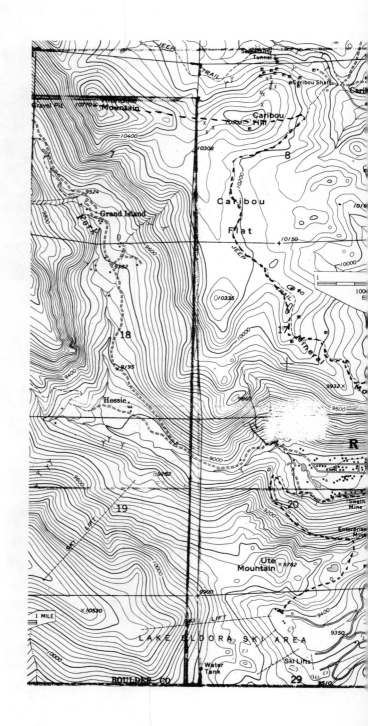

64

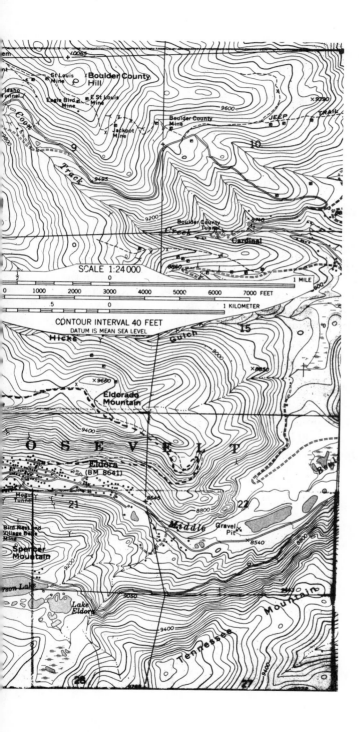

SCALE 1:24 000

1000 2000 3000 4000 5000 6000 7000 FEET

5 0 1 KILOMETER

CONTOUR INTERVAL 40 FEET
DATUM IS MEAN SEA LEVEL

through a beautiful forest to just below the summit of Mineral Mountain (9,932 feet). From here it goes north to cross Caribou Flat and west of Caribou Hill.

From here, there is no trail, but since you are now above timberline, you can easily see the path to follow to climb Caribou Hill (10,502 feet). From Caribou Hill, drop down about 100 feet, and then climb an additional 370 feet to make Klondike Mountain (10,770 feet).

Elevation gain from Eldora to Mineral Mountain: 1,291 feet

Elevation gain from Eldora to Caribou: 1,861 feet

Elevation gain from Eldora to Klondike: 2,129 feet

Spencer Mountain: For a shorter, scenic hike past a mine and over the ridge for a good look at the Lake Eldora ski area, turn south in the center of town where The Hitchin' Post is on the northwest corner of the street. Drive in along this road to the south and then west for about .5 mile to where you will reach a clearing for parking a couple of cars.

From this point, the road climbs through a forest to curve around Spencer Mountain (9,639 feet). Upon reaching the three forks in the road, keep to the left each time.

The road continues on to descend into the northeast side of the Lake Eldora parking lot.

Round trip distance: approximately 4 miles

Elevation gain: 800 feet

Elevation loss: 200 feet

Jasper Lake-King Lake Loop

This is a very strenuous, but fantastically beautiful hike for those with great endurance. You have the option of either visiting three mountain lakes in one loop, or taking a longer hike involving more elevation gain and visiting all eight lakes in the area. Either choice is quite rewarding.

Since Corona Pass is below one of the busiest air routes in the area, there undoubtedly will be many planes to witness your climbing feat.

To reach the trailhead, take Highway 119 to the Eldora turn-off southwest of Nederland. Drive 1.5 miles and keep to the right, as the Lake Eldora road forks left. Continue on through the town of Eldora and onto a dirt road. Keep to the left upon reaching the fork for the 4th of July road. After about a mile, you will reach a small parking area near the old town site of Hesse.

This section of the road leading from the turnoff into Hesse is extremely rough and rocky and is often under water, so caution

View shows King Lake in the foreground. Skyscraper Reservoir is the other large lake located to the right. The Continental Divide section of the trail, shown on the left side of the picture, shows the hiker more clearly that he needs to stay along the ridge until passing the second cirque before starting down to King Lake

Cabin below Jasper Lake

should be exercised. Many hikers prefer to park and walk this section.

From here continue to the west on foot along the old jeep road, crossing a bridge over North Fork Creek. Continue climbing, passing the turn-off to Lost Lake. After approximately .2 mile from here, you cross a bridge to the right to reach the fork for King Lake and Jasper Lake. Follow the trail to the right for 4.2

Jasper Lake

miles to Jasper Lake. This lake has a concrete spillway which you will cross.

Continue to the west on to Devil's Thumb Lake (.8 mile). From here, continue to follow the trail as it goes west, climbing steeply up to the Continental Divide. This divide walk is exceptionally beautiful in the fall since there are several springs on top making the tundra quite lush.

Continue hiking south along the top of the Divide for about 3 miles, watching for the Corona Pass Road. This road is also called the Rawlins Pass Road. As soon as you can see the remains of the old restaurant-hotel on top of the pass, begin looking for the trail heading northeast back down into the valley to King Lake. The trail bypasses King Lake, and continues back to the original trail fork.

Round trip: approximately 15 miles
Elevation gain: approximately 3,000 feet

Devil's Thumb Lake

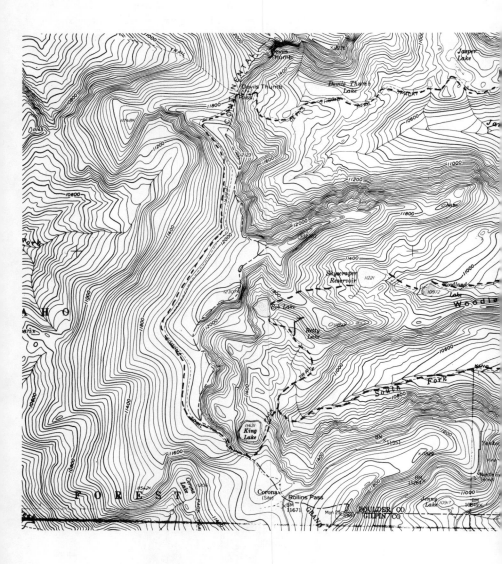

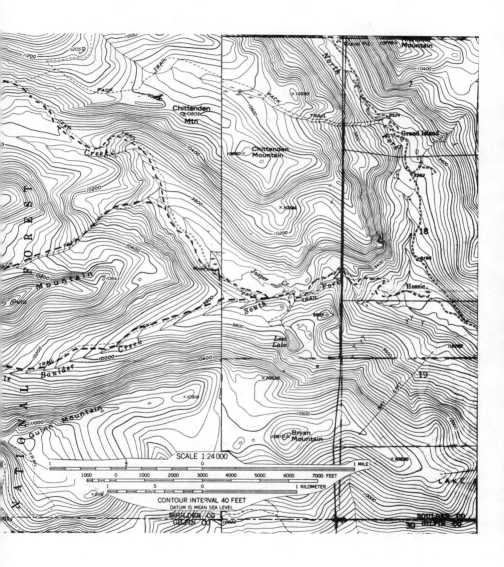

CONTOUR INTERVAL 40 FEET
DATUM IS MEAN SEA LEVEL

SCALE 1:24 000

71

King Lake

Betty and Bob lakes

Skyscraper Reservoir and Woodland Lake shown further to the west

If you should decide to visit all of the lakes in the area, take this hike as described until you pass King Lake. The aerial photo should be of assistance in the rest of the traverse. Wind down from King Lake and cross the stream. After 1 mile, and just beyond this creek, there is a faint path off to the left that follows the stream bed for a short distance. Go to the right and continue climbing to the southeast end of Betty Lake.

To reach Bob Lake, go across the inlet creek from Betty Lake. Stay along the southwest shore, and then, keeping the inlet creek from Bob Lake on your right, continue climbing to the south shore of Bob Lake.

From here a topographical map is quite helpful since there is no trail to Skyscraper Reservoir. Climb east over the ridge. Once on top of the ridge, you can see Skyscraper Reservoir. Go around the southeast side of it and watch for the trail on the northeast corner of the lake. This trail will take you back to Woodland Lake. There is a good-trail the remainder of the way back to the original King Lake fork and back to your car.

Total round trip distance: approximately 15 miles

Jenny Lind Gulch

Jumbo Mountain

The access to this area is through private property, so hiking through the beginning part of the area is not guaranteed.

To reach the trailhead, drive approximately 20 miles to Rollinsville from Boulder either via Highway 119 through Nederland, or take Highway 93 to its intersection with Coal Creek Canyon. Follow Coal Creek Canyon west to where it meets Highway 119 coming from Nederland, and turn south, following the road for a short distance to Rollinsville. The Rawlins Pass, or Corona Pass Road, turns west from here.

Drive on the Rawlins Pass Road for 4.0 miles. Here you will see a barbed-wire gate and a green and white sign posted on a tree off the road to the south which says, "No vehicles, camping or fires." The turn-out in front of this area will take only a few cars. Park here and follow the jeep road to the south.

After you reach the first fork in the road, keep to the right, since the left fork goes to private property. Continue hiking south for approximately one mile. Soon you come to a small creek which crosses the road, and another road turns right going west. Stay with the road heading south, crossing the stream. Here the road begins to climb more steeply. At the next fork, stay to the right. Continue climbing south until you are just about out of the trees. From here the road turns east for a short distance before going north.

At this point, you can see all kinds of jeep roads crisscrossing the mountain. If you stay with the road going northeast, you can climb Jumbo Mountain (9,959 feet).

Distance to Jumbo one way: approximately 4 miles
Elevation gain: 1,165 feet

Should you decide to take the road going east and climbing the hill, you will come to the next ridge on which there is an old mine and some old cabins. The road then continues to the Tip Top Mine.

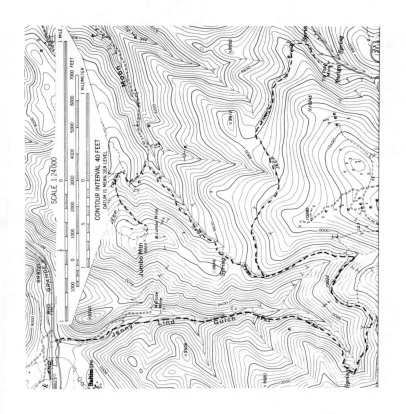

Jenny Lind Gulch trailhead

Old mining shack at Jenny Gulch

Old mining equipment found in Jenny Lind
Gulch

Golden Gate Park

Black Bear

Horseshoe

Buffalo

Burro

Blue Grouse

Ground Squirrel

Mule Deer

Elk Trail

Coyote

Raccoon

Goat

Golden Gate Loop Hikes

Golden Gate State Park is located about one hour from Boulder via Highway 93 to the north of Golden where you turn west onto Highway 70. Another route is to leave Boulder via Highway 119 up Boulder Canyon and continue with this road through Nederland as it goes south. This road also connects with Highway 70, which takes you to Golden Gate Park.

There are many trails in the area, all of which have been marked with animal tracks. The elevation of the area ranges from 7,600 to 10,400 feet.

This is an area that doesn't appear to be very well known. During the time the area was checked out, there were few other hikers there. The area is heavily wooded and has some good high

Golden Gate Aerial: Kriley Pond is in the foreground with Slough Pond just below. The road circling the mountain is Mountain Base Road. Blackman Meadow is in the upper left.

points from which to view the surrounding terrain. It also has some old cabins in some of the meadows, which are fun to explore.

Upon entering the park, you must purchase either a daily park pass for $2.00 or an annual pass for $5.00.

The trails may be walked individually for shorter hikes, or combined with others, making longer hikes.

Southern Trailheads

A. Black Bear Trail: The trailhead is located at Ralston Roost, .3 mile from the Visitor's Center at the east side of the park. This is one of the most difficult trails in the park because of its steepness, and goes 1.1 miles one way to Ralston Roost.

Elevation gain: 1,000 feet

B. Horseshoe Trail: The trailhead is at Ralston Creek which is .1 mile east of the Black Bear Trail. The trail winds upward for 2.3 miles where it comes in to Blackman Meadow near some old cabins. Rated easy.

Elevation gain: 800 feet

Golden Gate Park: Black Bear Trail signpost

C. Buffalo Trail: Begin at Red Barn Trailhead or continue around the corner on the road to the Knotts Pond Trailhead. The trail climbs 1,000 feet, passing a pond and more abandoned cabins, ending up at the group camp site at Rifleman Phillips Trailhead on Gap Road.

Distance: 3.0 miles one way

Black bear footprint used on trail post

Horseshoe Trail

D. Burro Trail: This one can be picked up either at the Bridge Trailhead or at the Red Barn Trailhead. The trail follows a service road for a short distance before heading north. It goes to some rock quarries for those of you who are rock hounds. This trail also follows a stream for a short time, and is quite delightful.

Distance one way: 3.5 miles
Elevation gain: 400 feet

Horseshoe trail marker

E. Blue Grouse Trail: One trailhead is at Slough Pond, .4 of a mile west of the Visitor's Center in the east part of the park, with the other one beginning at Kriley Pond. The trail climbs the hill to where it intersects Ground Squirrel Trail. The forest land on top is quite peaceful, since it is so deserted.

Distance one way: 2.3 miles
Elevation gain: 1,134 feet

F. Ground Squirrel Trail: This trail begins at Kriley Pond west of the Visitor's Center and climbs to Blackman Meadow.

Distance one way: 2 miles
Elevation gain: 800 feet

Blue Grouse and Ground
Squirrel meet here

follow blue grouse
track 2.3 miles
(3.7 kilometers) to
Ralston Roost
up 800 feet
(244 meters) elevation

HORSES PROHIBITED

MOTORIZED USE PROHIBITED

2.3 mi
3.7 km

800 ft
244 m

Blue Grouse trail sign

Kriley Pond trailhead

trail symbols

easy

moderate

difficult

campsites

distance

elev. change

Regulations
to help us serve you

1. Backcountry campground permit required
   for all overnight use. Obtain at
   visitor center.
2. All fires in backcountry are prohibited
   unless fire permit is obtained at
   visitor center.
3. All trash must be packed out of
   backcountry.
4. Tree cutting is prohibited for firewood
   or shelter construction.
5. Pets must be on a 6' leash at all times.
6. Vehicles must have a valid parks pass at
   all times.

Kriley Pond trailhead for Ground Squirrel Trail

Ground Squirrel sign

Close-up of Ground Squirrel
footprint

Western Trailheads

A. Mule Deer Trail: This trail begins at Mountain Base Trailhead on the east side of the road and continues to Blackman Meadow. After crossing the meadow, it terminates at Gap Road.

Distance: 3.0 miles one way
Elevation gain: 1,000 feet

B. Elk Trail: This can be picked up on the west side of Mountain Base Road at the Mountain Base Trailhead. It passes Bootleg Bottom on the west side, and ends up at Gap Hole near Reverend's Ridge Campground. To reach the campground, the trail meets the Raccoon Trail which comes from behind the visitor's center.

Distance one way: 3 miles
Elevation gain: 1,000 feet

Elk Trail signpost

Elk footprint trail marker

C. Coyote Trail: This begins at Bootleg Bottom. It climbs through an aspen-pine forest to the top of the ridge, where the hiker gets a good overlook of the mountains to the west. The trail at the top of the ridge is definitely a "heads up" situation, since it crosses some rocks. Watch for the trail continuing off to the north.

Distance one way: 2.2 miles
Elevation gain: 1,313 feet

HORSES PROHIBITED

MOTORIZED USE PROHIBITED

follow coyote
track 2.2 miles
2.2 mi / 3.5 km
(3.5 kilometers) to
Blackman Meadow
+ 900 ft / 274 m
up 900 feet
(274 meters) elevation
to backpackers
campground

Coyote signpost

D. Raccoon Trail: This begins east of the Reverend's Ridge Campground Headquarters. It goes down to the creek and then climbs back up to the east for an overlook area at Panorama Point. There you will find two good displays pointing out all of the mountains visible from this point.

Distance one way: 1.3 miles
Elevation gain: 200 feet

Raccoon trail marker

Eastern Trailhead

A. Goat Trail: If you begin at the Aspen Meadow Campground, you can take this trail for a short distance to Dude's Fishing Hole. If you continue northwest, you will intersect either Raccoon Trail, a short distance from Panorama Point, or Elk Trail going to the south.

Distance: 2 miles
Elevation gain: approximately 400 feet

Golden Gate Loop Hikes

A. Begin on Horseshoe Trail and follow it to its intersection with Coyote Trail in Blackman Meadow. The Coyote Trail then climbs to 9,200 feet before returning to the Bootleg Bottom picnic area. You might wish to stop for lunch there.

After lunch, cross the Mountain Base Road heading west to where Elk Trail comes in. Take this trail south down to a meadow with an old mining cabin. Watch for the trail continuing east from here, staying on the north side of the road.

Once you reach Mountain Base Road again, pick up Mule Deer Trail, and then take Ground Squirrel Trail back to Horseshoe Trail and out.

Distance round trip: approximately 11 miles
Elevation gain: approximately 3,100 feet

B. Begin at Bootleg Bottom picnic area. Pick up the Elk Trail going north to where it meets Goat Trail. Then intersect Mule Deer Trail near Gap Road near Lazy Squaw and follow it through Blackman Meadow to Mountain Base Road. Cross the road and pick up the southern end of Elk Trail.

Distance round trip: approximately 8 miles
Elevation gain: approximately 2,400 feet

Goat Trail in winter

Panorama Point overlooking the Continental Divide

C. Beginning at Reverend's Ridge Campground on the Raccoon Trail, follow Raccoon to the bottom of the hill where it intersects Elk Trail. Take Elk Trail to Goat Trail. Stay with Goat Trail as far as Gap Road. Then hike to the right along Gap Road for a short distance until reaching Panorama Point. Return to the campground via Raccoon Trail.

Distance round trip: approximately 5 miles
Elevation gain: approximately 400 feet

Cabin in Black Man Meadow

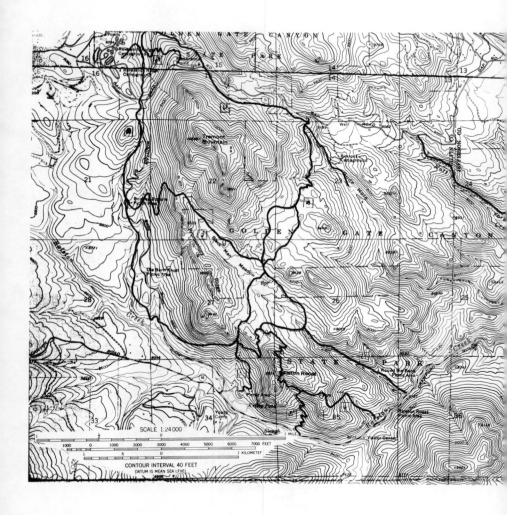

SCALE 1:24 000

1000	0	1000	2000	3000	4000	5000	6000	7000 FEET

CONTOUR INTERVAL 40 FEET
DATUM IS MEAN SEA LEVEL

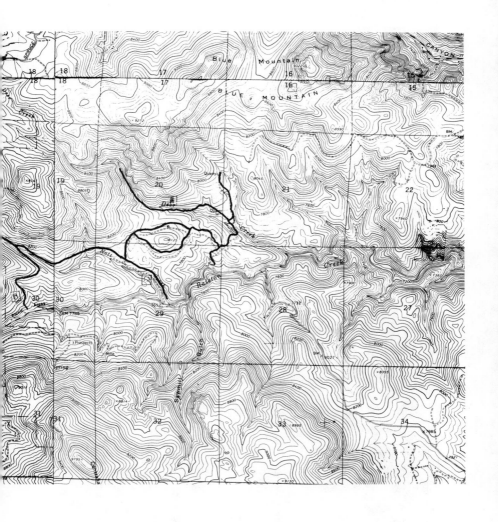

Left Hand Canyon Trails

Public Access

Nugget Hill

The Boulder foothills are full of old mining roads that criss-cross in many places, offering some very scenic hiking. Since many of these roads are quite steep, hiking boots can make a safer hike.

Public Access Road-Left Hand Canyon: This is a steep, old mining road that takes the hiker up to a good rock overlook of the plains to the east. It passes by several old mines along the way.

To reach the jeep road, take Highway 36 toward Lyons. Turn west by the Greenbriar Restaurant onto Highway 61. Continue 2.6 miles to the Buckingham picnic area. Turn right again. The Public Access Road is about 1 mile from Buckingham Park on the north side of the road.

Public Access Road. The road bypasses several mines before curving back to climb to the rocky overlook at the top of the mountain.

Road winds through a beautiful forest

Since this road is also used frequently by motorcyclists, it has many side trails going off in different directions, making it necessary for the hiker to keep track of landmarks in order to return to the car.

Once on top, the hiker has a good selection of rocks to scramble on, and from which to enjoy a tremendous view while eating lunch. If you continue to follow the road along the top, you will reach private property.

Distance round trip: 7.5 miles
Elevation gain: approximately 700 feet

Nugget Hill: This is another steep, yet picturesque mining road. To reach its beginning, located 14 miles from Boulder's northern city limits, take Highway 36 toward Lyons. Upon reaching the Greenbriar Restaurant, turn west onto Highway 61. Continue for 2.6 miles to the Buckingham picnic area. Now turn right. After 2.8 miles, you will come to another intersection. Take the left turn for Ward (Highway 106). After 3.8 miles, you will come to the old dirt mining road which is located just outside of the town of Rowena. This town is not marked in any way, but has several houses clustered there.

Nugget trailhead: Crucial that the hiker find this black miner's box to be sure of being on the right road.

After you have crossed the bridge just outside the town, watch for four mailboxes off to your right. They are just below an old large black box placed by the miners along the side of the road.

This road takes the hiker by several old mines. At the first major intersection, take the road going to the left. The right-hand fork will take you to another old mine. Then upon reaching the shoulder, the road again forks. Take the right-hand road going uphill and to the east. This road crosses one ridge and then drops down for a short distance before climbing to the top of Nugget Hill.

This is a good fall hike because there are many aspen trees along the ridge. It might be a good one to avoid in the late spring during tick season.

Round trip: 5 miles
Elevation gain: 1,362 feet

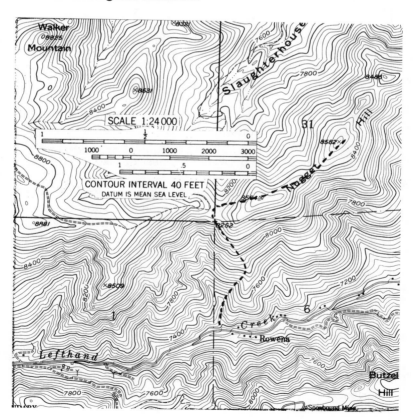

Switzerland Trail of America and Sugarloaf Mountain

Switzerland Trail of America: This is an old track bed of a railroad route built by the Colorado and Northwestern Railroad in 1898. Starting in Boulder, its route ran westerly to the intersection of Boulder and Four Mile Creeks. From here, it ran northwest, passing Crisman, Salina, Wall Street, Copper Rock, and then into Sunset.

At Sunset, the line divides, with one branch going to Eldora and the other to Ward. On the latter route, the train passed by or close to most of the most valuable mining claims of Boulder County.

Since this is an old railroad bed, the grade is quite gradual, making hiking quite enjoyable.

Accesses to this trail include the following:

1. Go up Boulder Canyon 5 miles to the Sugarloaf turn-off. Follow Sugarloaf Road uphill until you reach its top and the pavement ends. This is another 4.2 miles. At this point you will see 6 mailboxes off on the north side of the road where another dirt road meets the Sugarloaf Road. Follow this road to the north, keeping to the right at the first fork, and continuing on to the west. After .8 of a mile, you will come to the Switzerland Trail.

If you park here, you can either hike to the left on the Eldora branch to reach Glacier Lake in 5.5 miles, or hike to your right to Sunset in 4 miles.

2. Go to Gold Hill via Sunshine Canyon. Upon reaching town, continue to the west for an additional 3 miles to another section of the Switzerland Trail. Here the Trail may be taken to the south for 1 mile to the Mount Alto picnic area, and an additional 3 miles to Sunset.

If you follow the Switzerland Trail to the north, you will have a fairly level 3½ mile hike around the side of the mountain. Toward the end of the hike, the road narrows, becoming a footpath that goes over a rockfall below the main road leading to Lefthand Canyon.

3. Go up Boulder Canyon to the Four Mile Canyon turn-off (2.4 miles). Drive 11 miles up Four Mile Canyon to Sunset. From here, you can hike 4 miles to Glacier Lake or 4 miles to Sugarloaf.

Sugarloaf Mountain. Sugarloaf is in the foreground. The Switzerland Trail circles Sugarloaf with the left side of the road going to Glacier Lake and the right branch going to Sunset.

4. Glacier Lake Access: Take Highway 119 from Nederland, heading north. When you reach the Sugarloaf turn-off, you are 2.5 miles from the Glacier Lake Road. The turn-off is marked by a Forest Service access sign on the east side of the highway.

The Glacier Lake area is one that was highly popular when the old narrow gauge railroad came from Boulder to the lodge at the lake. Unfortunately, the lodge has since been gutted by fire, but the old stone walls and old fireplace in the courtyard still remain.

If you hike from Glacier Lake to Sunset, the distance is 9.5 miles. This hike might be a good one for a car key exchange.

Sugarloaf Mountain: To reach this mountain, take Boulder Canyon west for 5 miles to the Sugarloaf turn-off. Follow the Sugarloaf Road up to the top of the hill where the pavement ends after about 4 miles. There you will find 6 mailboxes beside a dirt road going to the north. Follow this road, keeping to the right at the one fork, and then continuing west for .8 of a mile. Park here near the Switzerland Trail and look for an unmarked mining road going uphill to the northeast. This road leads to a fantastic overlook of the mountains to the west and the valley to the east. The Arapaho Indians used this lookout as a signaling point.

Distance: 1 mile one way
Elevation gain: 476 feet

Glacier Lake. Highway 119 is at the bottom, and the Switzerland Trail is on the right.

Glacier Lake

Old lodge at Glacier Lake where the Switzerland Trail ride once dropped picnickers. Now located on private property.

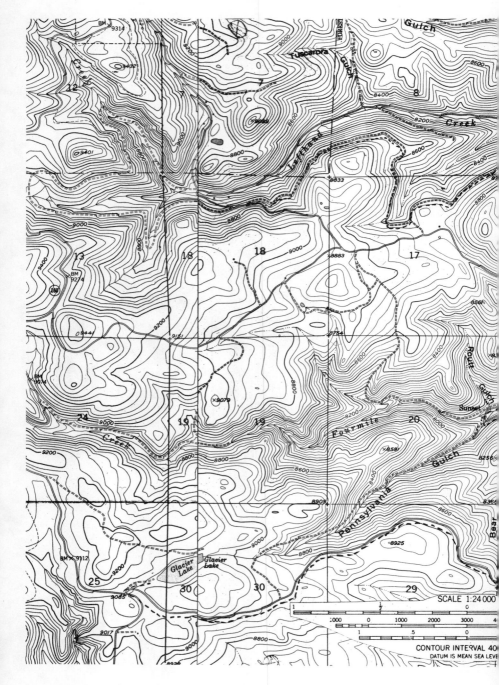

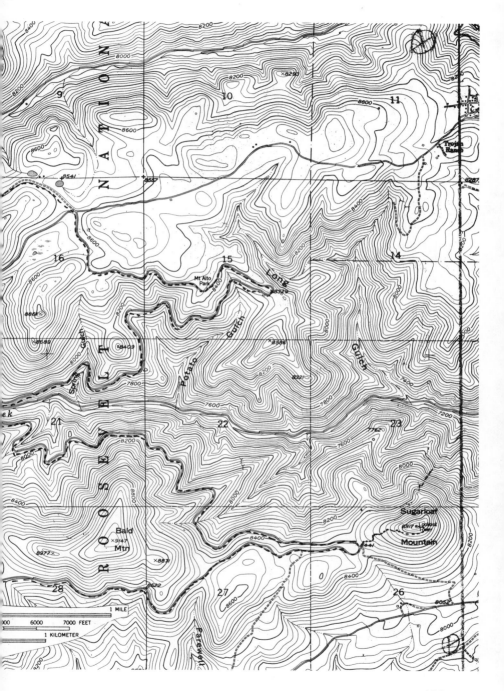

Thorodin Mountain

To reach the trailhead, take Highway 93 out of Boulder to Highway 72, Coal Creek Canyon. Follow Coal Creek to the west. Upon reaching the Coal Creek Canyon Inn, you are 2 miles west of the turn-off for Thorodin. The trailhead is 19 miles from Boulder.

Turn south on Camp Eden Road and follow this road until it dead-ends at the Axton Ranch. Since this is private property, permission should be obtained from the owner of the ranch at 642-3414.

The trail climbs through a forest, bypassing some good raspberry-picking bushes. Once on top, you reach the fire lookout as well as a picnic table where you can have your lunch. The hike offers some good views of the plains and mountains, and gives a good idea as to why a fire lookout was placed on its top.

Round trip: 6 miles
Elevation gain: 1,500 feet

The Axton Ranch: Thorodin Mountain trailhead

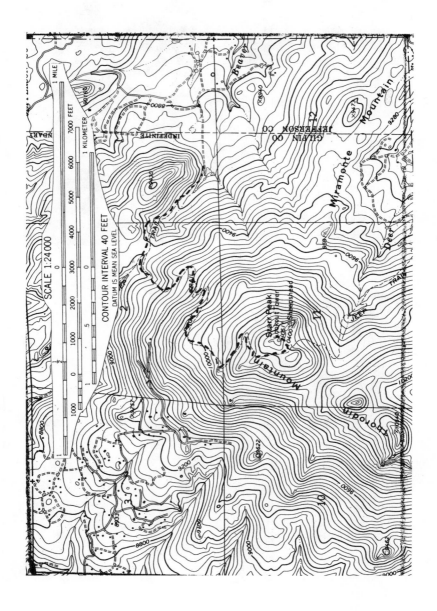

Trail marker for Thorodin

Road portion of the trail

Walker Ranch

Boulder Creek

Scenic Loop

Meyers Gulch

The recently acquired Walker Ranch, located on Flagstaff Road, offers 2,690 additional acres of open space for hikers. The land was originally homesteaded by James Walker in 1873; the present ranch house was built in 1898.

To reach the ranch, take Baseline Road west to Flagstaff Road. When the Flagstaff Road turns east to go to the summit of the mountain, stay with the Kossler Lake Road going west, passing Kossler Lake. The acreage is just beyond Pine Needle Notch, 7.4 miles from Baseline Road.

Walker Ranch parking area. The road inside the fence leads down to Boulder Creek.

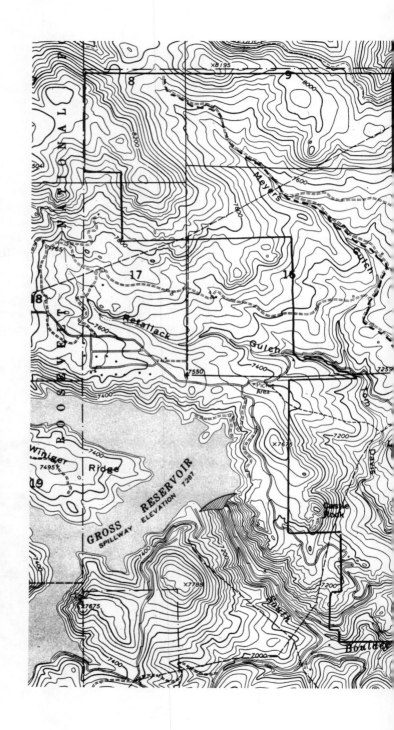

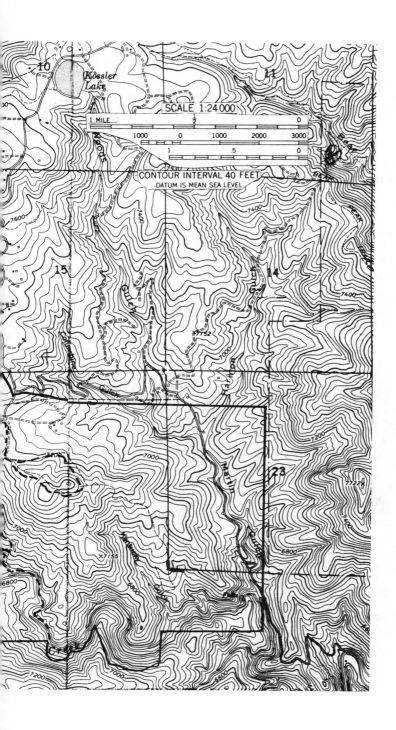

SCALE 1:24 000

1 MILE

1000   0   1000   2000   3000

1   5   0

CONTOUR INTERVAL 40 FEET
DATUM IS MEAN SEA LEVEL

Boulder Creek: For those looking for a hike along a stream to enjoy the restful sounds of running water, and perhaps to do a little fly fishing, park at the gate to the entrance to the property and take the road heading west. Continue through the fenced area and head downhill for just over a mile to reach Boulder Creek. This road then continues along the stream bed for a short distance before coming to an end at a washed-out bridge.

Round trip: approximately 4 miles
Elevation lost and regained: 600 feet

Scenic Loop: Another short but scenic loop may be taken by following the road from the gate off to the west until past the fence. Instead of continuing straight ahead to the west, follow the road south along the fence line and then climb to the top of the ridge for a good view of the forested mountains to the west as well as of the fire lookout atop Thorodin.

Round trip: 2.4 miles
Elevation gain: approximately 200 feet

Boulder Creek: scene of good fly fishing

Meadow at end of Meyers Gulch

Meyers Gulch: For a walk to a good overlook, take the dirt road across the Kossler Lake Road and north of the Walker Ranch. This road goes past a working mill where the hiker should keep to the right. After .5 mile, the hiker will reach another fork in the road. The dirt road going off to the right and to the east climbs up to a ridge and a gate where two homes have been built. By continuing left with the road to the northwest, you'll pass through a beautiful forest before coming out at the overlook where the road dead-ends.

For those who like to scramble around on rocks, there are some good ones at the fork where the road goes off to the east. If you stay on the left fork for a short distance, you can see poles installed on the hill to the east. This hillside is steep, but the view and the rock scrambling make it worth the effort.

Distance to overlook: 2.75 miles
Elevation gained: 600 feet

Note: The boundaries of the ranch property are marked on the map since the property surrounding the area is privately owned.

White Ranch

Rawhide

Wranglers Run

Waterhole

Belcher Hill

Mustang

Sawmill

Maverick

Longhorn

Jefferson County Open Space includes a very scenic park just 25.2 miles from Boulder. The area was originally home-steaded by the White family in the 1900s and served as a cattle ranch from 1903-1969.

The trails in the area go in various loops, making it possible for the hiker to take as long or as short a hike as time and desire permit without having to retrace any footsteps.

To reach White Ranch, drive toward Golden on Highway 93 to its intersection with Highway 56 (15.6 miles from Table Mesa Drive). Turn west onto the Golden Gate highway and continue to Crawford Gulch (3.9 miles farther). Turn right onto Crawford Gulch and continue for 4 more miles. Turn right again and pro-ceed 1.4 miles to the entrance to White Ranch. The main parking area, complete with picnic tables and rest facilities, is 1.5 miles from the gate.

From the parking area, the hiker has many possibilities. All of the trails are over varying terrain with some very steep expo-sures. The elevation difference on the western side of the ranch is approximately 650 feet. The trails here are through beautifully wooded areas where a large herd of deer may be seen roaming.

After exploring the western loops, the hiker may wish to return to the picnic area for lunch before looking over the eastern trails. To pick up the Belcher Hill Trail, hike west along the entrance road for .3 of a mile. It begins on the south side of the road. From here, descend through the woods to some small creeks. To get an overview of the entire ranch, continue with the Mustang Trail and return to the parking lot via Longhorn Trail (6.4 miles). The maximum elevation loss on this side is approximately 1,480 feet.

Trails on the White Ranch

Should the hiker wish to make a little shorter loop but still have a good view of this extremely scenic area, the loop from Belcher Hill to Mustang Trail down to where it joins Belcher Hill and then back to Maverick and to Longhorn offers another good hike of 5.1 miles.

The trails in the eastern section have many good open viewing points where the hiker can see Ralston Reservoir out to the north as well as the various mesas out to the east.

Jefferson County has located many of these trails on the perimeter of the ranch so that the hiker can better view the wildlife in a natural setting without disturbing them. Since the diamondback rattlesnake may also be found in the park, caution should be employed around rock and rubble piles where the snakes may be found during the warmer months of the year.

Because the trails cover much steep terrain, drinking water should be carried.

White Ranch Trails
1. **Rawhide 4.2 miles**
2. **Wranglers Run .8 miles**
3. **Waterhole .6 mile**
4. **Belcher Hill 2.5 miles**
5. **Mustang 2.3 miles**
6. **Sawmill .6 mile**
7. **Maverick .9 mile**
8. **Longhorn 2.7 mile**
Outer loop of the property: 10 miles

Old log near cattle pens on the ranch

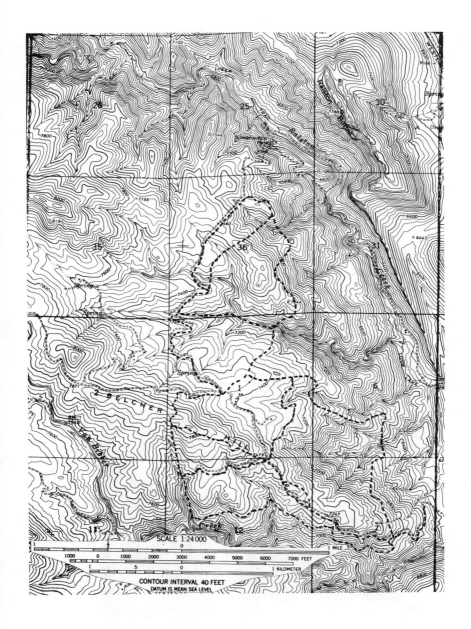

SCALE 1:24 000

CONTOUR INTERVAL 40 FEET
DATUM IS MEAN SEA LEVEL

Upper Forest Lake Via
Jenny Creek and Rollins Pass

The trails in the South Fork Middle Boulder Creek area (East Portal) are now difficult to reach from the former access from East Portal. The entrance to the lakes is now being leased by the International Sportsman's Club and permission may no longer be given for hikers to pass through their private property to reach the forest land above.

In 1983, Colorado Mountain Club was continuing to conduct negotiations with the sportsman's club in an effort to regain access to the area. In the meantime, you can reach the upper Forest Lake from the Lake Eldora Ski Area via the Jenny Creek Trail.

Park in the lower parking lot of the Lake Eldora ski area by the ski touring ticket office. Climb the hill beside the Ho Hum chairlift. Once on the top of the ski hill, turn right and follow the Foxtail ski trail as far as Upper Bunnyfair ski trail, located just below the large hill west of you.

Watch for the forest access signs and follow their trail through the woods, over a ridge, dropping down into Jenny Creek. Turn right onto the Jenny Creek jeep road and follow it towards the west, keeping Jenny Creek on your left.

Jenny Lake seen from the top of the 6.5 mile trail.

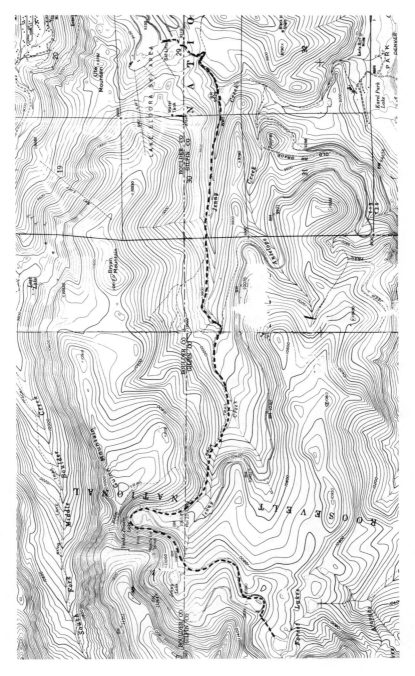

115

After approximately 3 miles you'll have to cross a tributary creek. Continue to the left when the road forks right to climb up to the Guinn Mountain Hut.

Follow the jeep road in a westerly direction. As you near Rollins Pass, the jeep road turns to the north and climbs above timberline to join Rollins Pass.

Once you've intersected the Rollins Pass road, you may wish to take a few minutes side trip to the northwest side of the road to take a look at Yankee Doodle Lake before proceeding on your way.

Turn left on the Rollins Pass Road and follow it past Jenny Lake, also on your right, to a hairpin turn in the road. Watch for a sign here on the right side of the road for Forest Lake. From here, there is no established trail for the last half mile down to the Upper Forest Lake. However, if you study the map and the picture, and look down to the southeast, you can soon see your destination.

Distance to lake: approximately 6.5 miles
Elevation gain: 1,727 feet
Elevation loss to the lake: approximately 200 feet

Shoshoni and Pawnee Peaks

Access to these peaks is from Indian Peaks. Drive in to Brainard Lake, off Highway 72, and take the fork to the Long Lake Trailhead.

Hike up the Pawnee Pass Trail to the pass. From here, you have the option of either hiking to the north up Pawnee Peak, bushwhacking your way to the top for 2,598 feet, or hiking to the south to climb up Shoshoni Peak.

Shoshoni doesn't have an established trail either, but since both peaks are above timberline, your route is easily picked. To climb Shoshoni from the pass entails hiking over some fields of talus up to the ridge below the peak. Once you're over the talus, the hike to the summit is along a grassy slope. The rocks on the summit only permit a small number of climbers to be there at one time.

To return from Shoshoni, you can drop down the grassy slopes and "skate" down some scree to the grassy meadows south of the Pawnee Pass Trail.

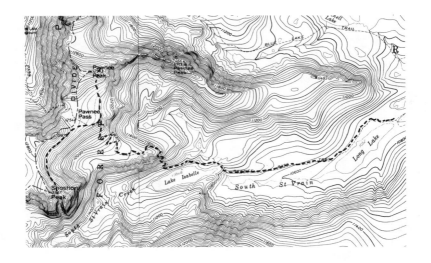

Distance up Pawnee Pass: 3.7 miles
Additional distance up Shoshoni: approximately 1 mile
Additional distance up Pawnee Peak: approximately .5 mile
Elevation gain up Shoshoni: 2,622 feet
Elevation gain up Pawnee Peak: 2,598 feet

Arapaho Pass "Knob"

For a truly beautiful lookout over the western valleys beyond Arapaho Pass, try this hike.

It begins from the 4th of July Campground reached by driving through the town of Eldora. When the road forks on the west side of town, turn right and drive up the rough dirt road to the recently constructed parking lot at the end of the road. Now you can also enjoy a newly built trail access to Arapaho Pass, replacing the one up the jeep road.

This trail crosses several streams and comes to some of the most breathtaking wildflower displays imaginable, as you wind your way up the switchbacks to the top of the pass. This hike is particularly colorful during July and August.

Once you come to timberline, you pass a trail forking off to your right, which goes up to an overlook of Arapaho Glacier and

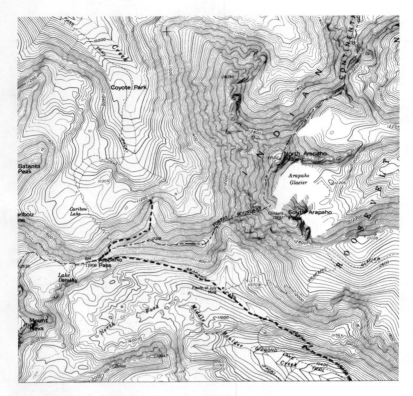

on to Arapaho Peak. Stay to the left here and continue to the top of the pass, passing Dorothy Lake on your left.

Once on the top of the ridge, continue to follow the pass to the west, dropping down a few hundred feet to a grassy knob off to your right. Turn to the north and follow this ridge north, crossing over some rocky outcrops until reaching the last one. This is a great place to enjoy both your picnic lunch as well as a tremendous overlook of Wheeler Basin at your feet. You can also get a good view of both North and South Arapaho Peaks as well.

Elevation gain: 1,676 feet
Distance: 2.8 miles to top of pass.
Additional 1 mile to knob overlook.

Caribou

To reach this old mining town, drive to Nederland via Boulder Canyon. Once in town, turn to the west onto Highway 72, the

Peak-to-Peak Highway, and continue for .3 mile to a marked turn to the west for Caribou.

This dirt road climbs for 5 miles up to 10,003 feet to the old town of Caribou. Not much is left of this town today except the old stone smelter.

Caribou was the site of a rich silver lode in 1869, and within a year after its discovery, the area was overrun with mines. Within a short time, over 3,000 inhabitants had moved in. At first they lived in tents, but gradually built wooden buildings.

The community boasted five saloons, and the two hotels: Planter's House and Sherman House, which were known from coast to coast for their fine meals.

The Caribou Mine was the richest one in the area, and in 1882, silver from the mine was used to pave a street in Central City. When President U.S. Grant visited Central City, he was able to step out of his carriage onto this silver path, laid especially for the occasion.

The town was wiped out twice by fire, once in 1879, and again in 1905. By then silver mining was declining because of the low price, and the town never recovered.

Along with the silver, the Caribou area sits on an iron dike, making it quite an attraction for summer electrical storms.

Ruins of the old mining town of Caribou.

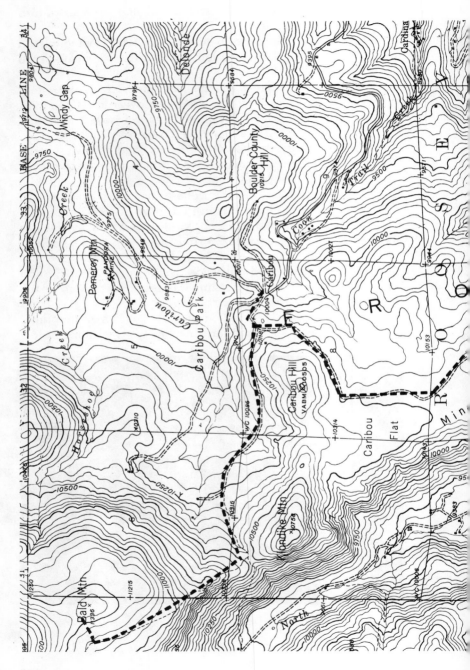

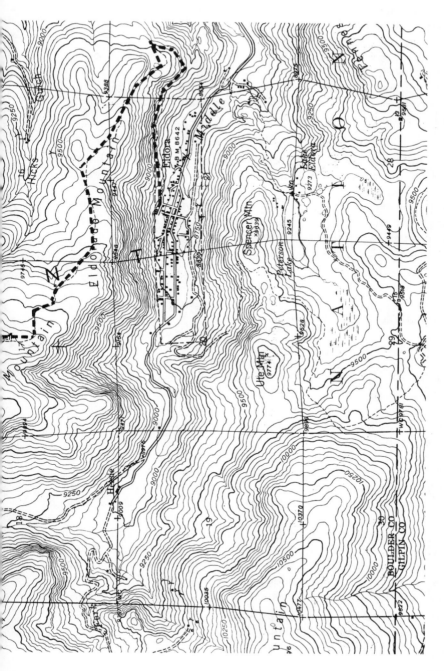

121

Because of its location, the area generally has snow for at least nine months of the year, and a pretty constant west wind.

Hiking in the area offers a couple of possibilities:

a. Park by the large sign. Hike along the jeep road going uphill to the south. This trail can be followed all the way to Caribou Flat which is also accessible from the town of Eldora. If desired, you could hike all the way over to Eldora, but you might wish to consider a car key exchange for this hike.

Distance to Eldora from Caribou: approximately 6 miles

b. Hike along the jeep road heading west. Upon reaching a fork in the road, turn right and head uphill to the north to climb Bald Mountain. The trail has one short, steep pitch, but otherwise is a gradual climb of 1332 feet. Once you're above timberline, you can see the old mine shack on the peak, and use this as a landmark when the trail peters out.

Distance up Bald Mountain: 3 miles
Elevation gain: 1,332 feet

Eldorado Springs

1. Eldorado Springs to Walker Ranch area.

Park at the entrance to Eldora Springs Park. Admission is charged for parking and for hiking within this state park.

The trail was under construction in 1983 and is scheduled to be completed as far as Pine Needle Notch by 1984. Plans for completing it on to the Walker Ranch Open Space property are already in the process.

The trail begins near the end of the dirt road going through the park. Where the road forks to a picnic area on the left, continue to the right a short distance, passing both the parking area with the historic trailhead, and the trail that goes up the draw on your right.

The new trail begins a short distance west of this draw and is below the gate marking private property. It's on the right side of the road and heads steeply uphill to the north. The trail has many switchbacks as it climbs steeply up, levels out, and then climbs up more to a magnificent view of the back range.

Distance one way: 4.5 miles
Elevation gain: 1,000 feet
Difficulty: intermediate

2. Hotel Ruins

For a shorter hike, go up to the old hotel ruins via Rattlesnake Gulch Trail. The hike begins approximately .5 mile up the dirt road from the parking area on the south side of the road. It's marked with a wooden signboard map of the area.

The trail begins gently and then begins to climb through the forest via some scenic switchbacks.

The view of the Continental Divide at the hotel ruin overlook is well worth the hike. The hotel itself has almost disappeared.

The trail has two forks going to the south which go up to the railroad tracks, but neither is marked by signs. However, both have rock cairns along the left side of the trail. The top one comes just before the overlook and ruins and has an arrow constructed of rock pointing back to the south. This trail is narrow, but easy enough to follow up to the tracks where the train enters a tunnel.

Distance: Hotel ruins: 1.9 miles
Overlook of Continental Divide: 3.1 miles
Elevation gain: 1,650 feet

Boulder Open Space

Boulderites are lucky to have access to 17,000 acres of open space land. Much of the land is undeveloped with no established trails as of 1983, with the exception of the Burke II property and the Sawhill Ponds. As future funds become available, perhaps we'll see the development of a comprehensive trail system connecting the various parcels of land which surround the city of Boulder. For now, hiking in these areas is mostly a do-it-yourself endeavor.

You will find old roads and overgrown trails in some areas. Since almost all the land is wide open with unrestricted views, you can easily pick your own path to explore.

Many historic fences still exist and these may be crossed. Most have been marked with open space signs. By looking at the map of the areas, you should be able to tell whether or not you're on open space or private land.

Hiking in some of the areas involves walking through tall grasses and native vegetation so long pants are advisable, particularly in the fall.

The ditches in the area are often full during the spring and summer, but should be dry during the fall.

The open space land is a great place to see birds and other wild animals in their native habitats, particularly at Sawhill Ponds. For hikers who enjoy hiking off trails, this is a good place to go without worrying about becoming disoriented.

The areas are not widely used for the most part, making it possible to hike away from the crowds usually found along the more popular trails.

Trail descriptions won't include distances or elevation gains since these will be determined by the individual hiker.

SDC: *Flatirons Vista:* Flatirons Vista has 475 acres.

Access is from Highway 93, 6 miles south of Boulder, and .3 mile past the intersection of Highway 93 and 128. The trailhead is unmarked from the road, so you need to watch for it. Park in the lot on the west side of the road where you see some old cattle chutes and a Boulder Parks open space bulletin board on the west side of the fence.

From here you can hike .9 mile west to the western park boundary. It's all private land west of this point. Now, you can either turn right and hike north along the fence .4 mile to an orange gate marking the entrance to the West Rudd Open Space property, or turn left and hike south along the fence, dropping down to the southern boundary. The hike north connects with two other open space areas where you get into some hilly terrain and do your own thing. There are no established trails until you drop down to the Community Ditch which is visible from this point.

If desired, you could hike west across the Rudd property all the way to the Dunn II property to another trailhead and picnic area. However, you'll lose quite a bit of elevation by doing so, and would have to wade across the ditch during the months when it's flowing.

If you hike to the south along the fence, you'll drop down a gully near a gravel mining operation. The open space property extends all the way to the south to the Jefferson County line, but as a hiker, you'll probably want to stay high along the ridge to return to your car. There is no established trail at this point, but the area is wide open and you can easily get back to Highway 93 by hiking out to the east and then back to the north.

To reach your car, you'll have to cross an historic fence a short distance south of the parking lot. An opening in this fence is close to Highway 93 near the lot.

An orange gate marks the entrance to the West Rudd Open Space.

East Rudd Property: Marshall Mesa: This open space land is 562 acres.

This land is directly east of the old hotel ruins. However, the established access is from Marshall Road, Highway 170. Drive east for .9 mile on Highway 170 to the parking area on the south side of the road.

As you hike up the mesa, you pass through several sedimentary formations including the Laramie Formation. This contains rocks that were deposited by the river which left behind much rock and mud. Then, trees and ferns grew along a shoreline of marshy lagoons.

West Rudd Property: This property has 504 acres.

This open space property is located west of the old Hornbook Hotel ruins on the west side of Highway 93, 5 miles south of town. The hotel itself is on private property, but if you follow the dirt road to the west, you'll see an old road on the other side of the fence which leads into the open space area.

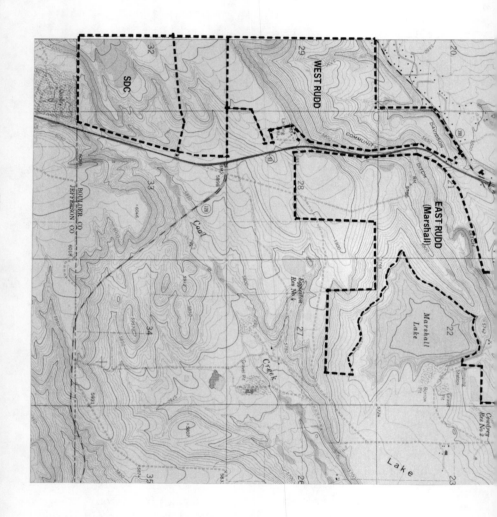

126

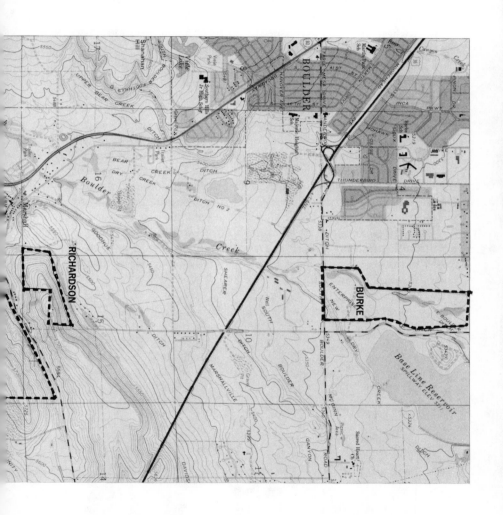

127

This road doesn't extend very far, so most hiking is strictly on your own. You can see the Community Ditch north of you, and the view to the west is totally unobstructed.

The land is leased for seasonal grazing.

Below the Laramie Formation is the Foxhills Formation which contains a number of fossils of oysters and clams left behind when the land lay beneath an inland sea. You may also spot some petrified wood here.

The Marshall area was mined in the 1800's, and in 1870, a spark from a campfire ignited a vein of coal at the back of one of the caves, setting the coal seam on fire. The fire continues to burn and in places the ground surface temperature reaches 300 degrees F. You may be able to see the smoke from this smoldering fire as you reach the top of the mesa and look around you.

Also while you're in the area, you may be able to spot some of the original powder caves that were even lived in by some of the early miners who were unable to afford any other housing. During 1910-1914, these slopes were used by soldiers who were posted there to protect "scabs" from the striking coal miners.

Although there are no established trails in the area, you can go through the gate and after a short distance, see a faint trail going to the east. This can be followed to the eastern fence line, a short distance from South 66th Street.

The trail across the West Rudd Property follows Marshall Ditch. Marshall Ditch.

Now you could turn south along the fence line and hike up the hillside to reach the ditch "trail" to do a loop to return to your car.

Another option: If you go up the hillside south of the parking lot, crossing Davidson Ditch and going on up to the ridge beside Community Ditch, you can hike west towards Highway 93.

Open space only surrounds Marshall Lake on three sides: the north, west and south. The east side is owned by the Louisville Rod and Gun Club. If the ditch isn't flowing, you could hike around the part of the lake owned by the city.

Most of the hiking in this area is through some tall grasses and native vegetation, and long pants can make the hike more enjoyable.

Richardson Property: This property has 66 acres.

This property is near the intersection of Marshall Drive and Cherryvale Road on the east side of Cherryvale. This area was also mined, and there are areas of subsidence as well as old mine pits, mine diggings and white cliffs. There is no established trail here, so if you visit here, you can do your own thing.

Burke II Property: This property has 191 acres.

This is one of the most scenic in-town acquisitions. The trailhead is off Baseline Road on the south side of the street, one block before you reach Cherryvale Road. Park in the lot on the south side of the street. Now you can hike along a trail which follows Boulder Creek through some beautiful cottonwoods which makes this a very shady, cool place to hike.

If you follow the trail south, staying along the creek for the first part, you'll soon reach a fork in the trail a few yards from a fence. If you go straight ahead, you'll dead-end at the fence. If you take the fork to the left, you'll come to a gate.

Now you can either extend your hike to the south along an old road which meets another fence about a half mile away. Open space extends south beyond this fence all the way to South Boulder if you want to cross the small ditch and fence to continue.

Otherwise, you can go south to the second fence and turn around. Upon returning to the gate, follow the trail in front of you, located east of the creek trail, to return to your car.

Present plans for the area include a 14 station self-guiding nature trail to be in place in 1984 along with a picnic area down by the creek.

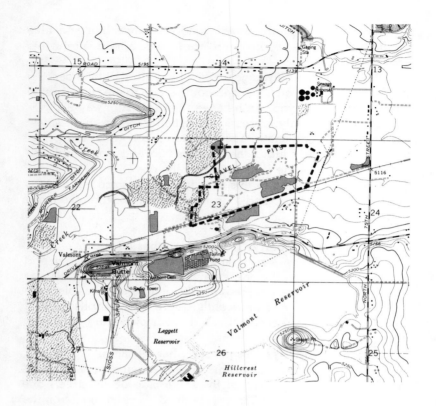

Sawhill and Walden Ponds Wildlife Habitats: These 15 ponds are located 9 miles east of Boulder. Drive east out Baseline Road to 75th and turn left. Head north, and after passing Jay Road, begin watching for the turn-off to the west approximately 1 mile further.

Boulder Creek's ancient floodplain once covered this area, leaving behind much sand and gravel. The gravel was mined from the area for almost twenty years, finally ending in the 1970's. Mining still goes in nearby areas. Following the mining, the ponds were left to become a wildlife habitat.

Senior citizens fish in the largest of the ponds.

The cottonwoods on the west side of the pools are just a few left behind from the many that once lined Boulder Creek. These form an ideal spot for many native shrubs, grasses and nocturnal animals such as coyotes, rabbits, raccoons, owls, skunk, squirrel and fox.

Bird watchers thoroughly enjoy these ponds since Colorado is located midway between the northern and southern breeding grounds of many waterfowl. You'll see many ducks on the ponds, both dabblers and divers. The dabblers, including mallards and teals, feed on the surface of the water, or on plants growing just beneath the water's surface. They feed by tipping over, with their tails held high in the air. The divers, whose legs are closer to their tails, dive beneath the water for their food.

The ponds have a self-guiding nature trail with signposts around some of the lakes. There were pamphlets available at one time, but these are now out of print.

Dunn II: This property covers 280 acres.

The Dunn II acreage is directly across the street from the southern end of the Mesa Trail. To reach it, take Highway 170 towards Eldorado Springs for 1.1 miles. The trailhead is on the south side of the highway.

A .3 mile trail leads to a picnic area and an old log cattle chute.

Any further hiking from this picnic area is strictly a do-it-yourself proposition. There are some faint equestrian trails which you can explore if desired.

If you decide to hike to the south, you will need to cross a ditch which may be running during the spring and summer. During the fall, you can easily cross it to get across to explore the other side.

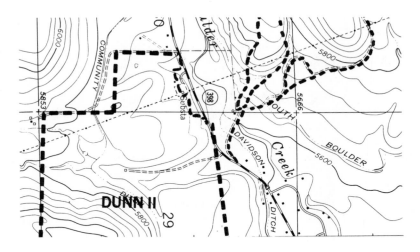

Summary of Trails

Trail	Distance From Boulder (in miles)	Elevation Gain (in feet)	Length of Trip, One Way (approximate, in miles)	U.S. Geol. Survey Maps
Allenspark Area				
Meadow Mountain	28	2,800	4.0	Allenspark
St. Vrain Mountain	28	3,332	5.5	Allenspark
Arapaho Pass Knob	22	1,676	3.8	Monarch Lake
Sunshine Canyon				
Bald Mountain Scenic Area	4.3	200	.25	Boulder
Betasso Preserve	6.2			
Bummer's Rock		270	.5	Boulder
Canyon Trail		400 (lost and regained)	2.5	Boulder
Boulder Mountain Parks				
Mesa Trail		600	6.0	Boulder, Eldorado Springs
Woods Quarry		250	.4	Boulder
NCAR		80	.5	Boulder
Enchanted Mesa		400	1.2	Boulder
McClintock Nature		400	.7	Boulder
Shanahan and Greenslope		640	1.6	Boulder
Bluebell-Baird		300	.8	Boulder
Chautauqua		280	.6	Boulder
Mallory Cave		700	.4	Boulder
Bear Cave		400	1.0	Boulder
Harmon Cave		400	.25	Boulder
Royal Arch		1,000	.9	Boulder
Bear Peak via Bear Canyon		2,200	3.2	Boulder
Bear Peak via Fern Canyon		2,100	1.3	Boulder
Bear Peak via Shadow Canyon		2,100	1.7	Boulder
Flagstaff		1,050	1.5	Boulder
Boy Scout		80	.6	Boulder
May's Point		80	.2	Boulder
Artist Point		40	.1	Boulder
Tenderfoot		1,000	1.5	Boulder
Ute		160	.5	Boulder
Plains Overlook		40	.3	Boulder
Range View		160	.5	Boulder
Gregory Canyon		800	1.2	Boulder
Saddle Rock		1,200	1.0	Boulder
Amphitheater		550	.5	Boulder
Greenman		1,500	1.5	Boulder
Ranger		1,450	2.3	Boulder

West Ridge		600	1.5	Boulder
Long Canyon		750	1.5	Boulder
Mount Sanitas		1,200	1.2	Boulder
Red Rocks		400	.5	Boulder
Aqueduct Trail		400	2.0	Boulder
Fire Road		200	1.5	Boulder
Boulder Open Space				
SDC: Flatirons	6.3			Louisville
East Rudd:				
Marshall Mesa	2			
West Rudd	5			
Richardson	2			
Burke II	2			Niwot
Sawhill and				
Walden ponds	9			
Dunn II	5		.3	Louisville,
				Eldorado Springs
Caribou-Bald				
Mountain	22.3	1,332	3.0	Nederland
Caribou-Eldora	22.3		6.0	Nederland
Eldorado Ski Area	21			
Bryan Mountain		1,523 via	2.5	East Portal,
		Cannonball		Nederland
		1,850 via	5.2	
		Jenny		
Guinn Mountain		1,807 via	4.0	
		Jenny		
Town of Eldora	24			
Mineral Mountain		1,291	3.0	Nederland
Eldorado				
Mountain		1,019	2.0	
Caribou Hill		1,861	5.5	
Klondike		2,129	6.0	
Spencer		800	2.0	
Eldorado Springs				
Mesa Trail	5.5			Eldorado Springs
a. Middle Trail			2.5 loop	
b. Towhee Trail			2.5 loop	
c. Straw Draw				
Trail			4.5 loop	
Eldorado Springs-				
Hotel Ruins	6	1,650	1.9	
Eldorado Springs-				
Walker Ranch	6	1,000	4.5	
East Portal	26			
Jasper Lake-				
King Lake		3,000	15.0	Nederland,
			(round trip)	East Portal
Jenny Lind Gulch-				
Jumbo Mountain		1,165	4.0	Nederland
Golden Gate Park				
Black Bear		1,000	1.1	Black Hawk,
				Tungsten
Horseshoe		800	2.3	
Buffalo		1,000	3.0	
Burro		400	3.4	

134

Blue Grouse		1,134	2.3	
Ground Squirrel		800	2.0	
Mule Deer		1,000	3.0	
Elk Trail		1,000	3.0	
Coyote		1,313	2.2	
Raccoon		200	1.3	
Goat		400	2.0	
Left Hand Canyon				
Public Access	14	700	3.7	Boulder
Nugget Hill	14	1,362	2.5	Boulder
Shoshoni and				
Pawnee Peaks	30.5			Ward
Shoshoni		2,622	4.7	
Pawnee		2,598	4.2	
Switzerland Trail				
of America	10			
Sugarloaf to				
Glacier Lake			5.5	Gold Hill, Ward
Sugarloaf to				
Sunset			4.0	
Gold Hill to				
Sunset			4.0	
Gold Hill to				
Left Hand				
Canyon			3.5	
Sunset to				
Glacier Lake			4.0	
Sunset to				
Sugarloaf			4.0	
Glacier Lake				
to Sunset			9.5	
Sugarloaf Mountain	10	476	1.0	Gold Hill
Thorodin Mountain	19	1,500	3.0	Tungsten
Upper Forest Lake				
via Jenny Creek	24	1,727	6.5	Nederland, East Portal
Walker Ranch	7.4			
Boulder Creek		600	2.0	Eldorado Springs
Scenic Loop		200	2.0	
Meyers Gulch		600	2.75	
White Ranch	25.2			
Rawhide		-400	4.2	Ralston Butte
Wranglers Run		0	.8	
Waterhole		200	.6	
Belcher Hill		1,000	2.5	
Mustang		600	2.3	
Sawmill		50	.6	
Maverick		280	.9	
Longhorn		600	2.7